Tragedy

Blackwell Introductions to Literature

This series sets out to provide concise and stimulating introductions to literary subjects. It offers books on major authors (from John Milton to James Joyce), as well as key periods and movements (from Old English literature to the contemporary). Coverage is also afforded to such specific topics as "Arthurian Romance." All are written by outstanding scholars as texts to inspire newcomers and others: non-specialists wishing to revisit a topic, or general readers. The prospective overall aim is to ground and prepare students and readers of whatever kind in their pursuit of wider reading.

Tragedy

A Short Introduction

Rebecca Bushnell

Blackwell
Publishing

BLACKWELL PUBLISHING

350 Main Street, Malden, MA 02148-5020, USA
9600 Garsington Road, Oxford OX4 2DQ, UK
550 Swanston Street, Carlton, Victoria 3053, Australia

First published 2008 by Blackwell Publishing Ltd

1   2008

Library of Congress Cataloging-in-Publication Data

Bushnell, Rebecca W., 1952–
Tragedy : a short introduction / Rebecca Bushnell.
p. cm.—(Blackwell introductions to literature)
Includes bibliographical references and index.
ISBN 978-1-4051-3020-2 (hardcover : alk. paper)—ISBN 978-1-4051-3021-9
(pbk. : alk. paper)
1. Tragedy—History and criticism.   2. Tragedy—History and
criticism—Theory, etc.   I. Title.
PN1892.B87 2008
809.2′512—dc22
2007008014

A catalogue record for this title is available from the British Library.

Set in 10 on 13 pt Meridien
by SNP Best-set Typesetter Ltd., Hong Kong
Printed and bound in Singapore
by Markono Print Media Pte Ltd

For further information on
Blackwell Publishing, visit our website at
www.blackwellpublishing.com

Contents

Illustrations

Acknowledgments

This book synthesizes 25 years of teaching and writing about tragedy. I am grateful to several generations of students at the University of Pennsylvania for sharing their insights about tragedy with me and for bearing with my musings on the subject. Most recently, I learned much from my students in English 229 in the fall of 2005 and those of English 16 in the fall of 2006. I have also been ably assisted by three thoughtful and conscientious research assistants: Thomas Lay, Anthony Mahler, and Yu-Chi Kuo. I also owe much to many colleagues, including all the contributors to *The Companion to Tragedy* published by Blackwell in 2005, and particularly Phyllis Rackin and Ralph Rosen. Finally, Emma Bennett of Blackwell has offered unflagging support for the project.

R.B.

Preface

The notion of a "short introduction" to tragedy may seem absurd. How could anything "short" cover the genre that has produced some of the greatest masterworks of Western literature, beginning with the Greeks and extending to the present day? But one could take a lesson here from tragedy's self-discipline, which compresses the welter of human experience into what is most significant and timely. The exercise of a short introduction allows both writer and reader to focus on the essentials.

For most twenty-first-century readers, tragedy is a text to be read or a subject in school. They find it alien or stuffy, even while they eagerly consume tragic material through television and film. The media of film and television thrive on the kind of violence, conflict, passion, madness, and catastrophe that tragedy first introduced to the stage in fifth-century Athens. But what does this hunger mean for the viability of Sophocles, Shakespeare, Racine, or Ibsen?

This short introduction to tragedy would hope to reinvigorate the reading of tragedy for readers who want to understand it and to feel its power, yet who often find the masterpieces of the genre too distant from their own language and world. In that sense, I would hope to make some of the more alien aspects of the genre accessible: for example, to explain that the formal conventions of classic tragedy, its set pieces and rhetoric, are instrumental to evoking conflict and tension. This little book also seeks, albeit through the written word, to restore some of the theatrical energy of these plays. It explores how these plays lived on the stages of the past, but also imagines how tragedy could be re-created in the new "enacted" media of the screen.

However, inevitably, this introduction to tragedy cannot pretend to cover all the manifestations of tragic drama from the Greeks to the present. Rather, in each chapter, the book considers selected case studies that exemplify the compelling qualities of the genre. It offers an overview of the basics of the evolution of tragedy as a theatrical genre from the Greeks to the present, in its staging, its formal qualities, its characteristic plots, and its types of heroes. Because it looks at tragedy over time, this book also grapples with tragedy's connection to the historical conditions that produced it, while it cannot relate the details of that history.

A few plays recur throughout the book as touchstones for many aspects of the art. It should surprise no one that these plays include Sophocles' *Oedipus the King* and *Antigone*; Aeschylus' *Oresteia*; Euripides' *The Bacchae*; Shakespeare's *King Lear, Hamlet*, and *Antony and Cleopatra*; Racine's *Phèdre*; Ibsen's *Hedda Gabler*; and (perhaps a little more surprising) Beckett's *Waiting for Godot*. Many other plays are discussed, of course, but I am sure I have missed many readers' favorites, and I can only say that I have written mostly about those texts that served best to tell my story. It is also quite clear that the book does not take account of the transformation of tragic themes in opera: here I can only acknowledge that opera is certainly an important strand of the inheritance of tragic drama, but the introduction was simply too short to include a consideration of it. However, film is included here, because the cinema extends the experience of tragic drama as a popular art. If tragedy has a foreseeable future, it will be on the screen, whether in the space of the cinema, television, or computer.

Similarly, unlike other scholars of tragedy, I have not extended this introduction to the study of the tragic in the novel. This study is more narrowly focused on what Aristotle understood as the distinctiveness of tragedy, as opposed to epic: it is an "imitation" and, in tragedy (like comedy), the works "imitate people engaged in action, doing things" (19). Novels and epics, while they may share the ethos and character types of tragic drama, engage only a reader. Their audience is not trapped before them, pressed to follow the action to its conclusion.

So this short introduction to tragedy does not provide all the answers or cover all the bases, but it does ask quite a few questions. Tragedy itself is a genre that poses questions about the fundamental matters of our lives, and it does not answer them. What I would hope is that when the reader puts down this book, he or she will be compelled to ask more of these masterpieces.

CHAPTER 1

Tragic Theaters

Imagine yourself in an amphitheater open to the sky, where you witness a human spectacle. Everything seems to depend on its outcome. The people you watch so intently are engaged in a struggle, matching their wit and strength. Everyone knows that in the end victory must come at the cost of another's defeat.

Surely by now you have conjured up a sporting event – no ordinary match, perhaps, but a World Cup football championship or the final game of the baseball World Series. But what if the scene were a play? What if the spectacle were not one of balls flying and limbs pumping, but of daggers, tears, embraces, and death? What difference would it make if you came not just to see bodies in action but also to *hear* words of joy and agony? Would you still feel that it mattered, that somehow, at that moment, your life was bound to those of the players?

These days we observe tragedy in the dark, less like a game and more like a private act, in the flickering light of the cinema or the gloom of the theater, unless we are sitting in our well-lit homes in comfortable chairs, transfixed by the television screen. Because we are in the dark, tragedy strikes us in our eyes, mind, and heart, but we tend not to feel it as a communal or shared experience.

But it was not always so. In classical Greece tragedy was performed in glorious outdoor amphitheaters. It was created to be played out in the open, before thousands of people, in full sight of earth and sky. In early modern England, tragedy also flourished outside in the amphitheaters of London, before audiences that mixed aristocrats and apprentices, as well as in the murky, roofed playhouses like the Black-friars Theatre and in the elegant halls of the court. But by the end of the seventeenth century in Europe, tragedy had moved permanently indoors, into the confines of a framed and increasingly realistic stage setting and a socially stratified playhouse. These new circumstances redefined the meaning of tragedy itself.

To begin to understand tragedy, one has to imagine it as a living art, especially as it began in the dazzling sunlight of ancient Greece. Throughout the history of tragic art in the West, from the Theatre of Dionysus to the contemporary cinema, the conditions of performance, including setting, acting style, staging, and the composition of the audience, have defined its cultural impact and significance. Most tragedy was written to be played in a theater and, as such, to be a sensory as well as mental experience. What Bert States has termed the theater's "affective corporeality" (the material conditions of performance) exists in tension with language to embody complex and often contradictory meanings (27). This chapter will endeavor to evoke a performance of a Greek play in the Theatre of Dionysus and then compare it with performances of Shakespearean tragedy in different London settings, the staging of French neoclassical tragedy in Paris, and a presentation of a play by Ibsen in a nineteenth-century proscenium theater. In each case the conditions of theatrical performance served to define the tragic experience. In the case of Greek and English Renaissance tragedy, performance informed the tensions of knowledge and belief, whereas in French neoclassical and realistic drama, it structured the tragic dynamics of freedom and imprisonment.

The Theatre of Dionysus and Athens

Most people never get a chance to see a Greek tragedy performed. They may read one in school as literature, more like a poem than as a play, for indeed, that is the way they can look on the page. But we should never forget that these were plays written to be performed in the spectacular open-air theaters of early Greece. These plays are *theater* and theaters are places for things to be seen (*theatron*), not for reading (see Taplin: 2).

Athenian society was fiercely competitive (this is, after all, the city that gave us the Olympics), and tragedy, too, was the product of a competition. Each year three playwrights fought to win the prize for the best tragedies performed at the City Dionysia, a state-sponsored spring festival in honor of the god Dionysus. Each playwright presented a set of four plays: three tragedies and a satyr play (a more comic and vulgar piece that commented on the themes of the preceding tragedies). Going to the theater was no casual night out. It was a marathon experience, important for the welfare of the city and the honor of its gods.

These festival performances were at once religious and profoundly civic in nature. The theater belonged to both Dionysus and the city of Athens, since the City Dionysia was supported by the state. The city's leaders or *archons* would appoint a wealthy sponsor or *choragus* who would fund the production of the plays for the city's benefit. The chorus's dances and lyric language certainly evoked the mystery and power of divinity, while the actors' words and gestures echoed the formal discourse of the law courts or assembly as well as the intimate language of the family. The performances may have begun with a procession in honor of Dionysus, but they also involved appearances by political figures and the display of symbols of the imperial might of Athens (see Boedeker and Raaflaub).

The Theatre of Dionysus still nestles on the southeast slope of the Acropolis, which looms over it as a monument to Athens' ruined splendor, and its original shape is still visible, although eroded by the centuries (and the round orchestra has been split into a semicircle) (see Illustration 1). In the fifth century BCE the audience sat on that hillside in a crowd that was between 15,000 and 20,000 strong. They were arranged in a semicircle overlooking a round *orchestra* or "dancing place." A chorus composed of amateur citizens in costume inhabited the orchestra, chanting and dancing, or sometimes standing in silence or mingling with the actors. At the back of the orchestra was a building called the *skene* (now long gone): this space belonged to the professional actors. They would enter the scene either from doors in the *skene* or from passageways or ramps (*eisodoi*) on either side when a character was understood as coming in from the country or traveling (see Illustration 2). Two kinds of stage machinery also provided access to the playing area: one was the *mechane* or machine, which would allow an actor to come flying onto the stage (thus giving rise later to the term *deus ex machina*, or "the god from the machine"), and the *ekkyklema*, a wheeled platform that could be rolled out from the *skene*, often for the display of bodies. The *skene* served not only as a place for the actors to change their costumes but also to represent interior space:

ILLUSTRATION 1   The site of the Theatre of Dionysus in Athens today. *Photo © istockphoto.com/Michael Palis*

the palace, cave, or hut from which the actors emerged into the public eye and to which they retreated, often to commit acts of terror while hidden from the audience. While it may have been decorated with painted cloths for dramatic effect, the primary function of the *skene* was to define unseen indoor space as opposed to the public space inhabited by the chorus (see Halleran).

Even while Greek tragedy was a spectacle to be *watched*, it was also notable for not showing the most horrific acts (in contrast to English Renaissance tragedy, which reveled in stage blood). Oliver Taplin has cautioned us about thinking that in the Greek theater the *action* takes place offstage, if you think that "action" is just battles and sea-fights: "This is to miss the point that the stuff of tragedy is the individual response to such events; not the blood, but tears" (160–1). The Greek audience did not experience horror through seeing unspeakable acts. Instead, the horror would erupt from anticipating or imagining violence, or in witnessing its emotional waste.

What did the audience actually see? They watched male citizens transformed into a chorus of 15 individuals, sometimes men and

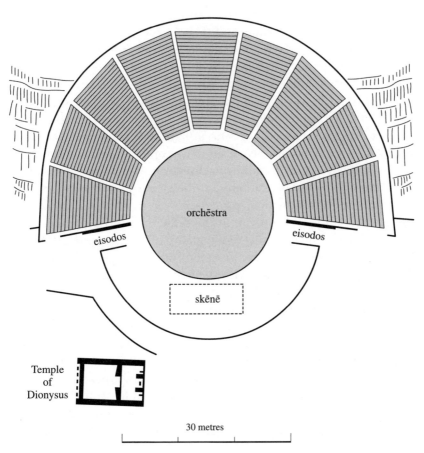

ILLUSTRATION 2 A schematic design of the Theatre of Dionysus, Athens, based on J. Travlos, *Pictorial Dictionary of Ancient Athens* (London, 1971), p. 50

sometimes women. The chorus entered after the opening scene and remained in the orchestra for the entire play, sometimes silent, sometimes speaking with the actors, and sometimes singing and dancing for the choral odes that separated the acts of the tragedy. Juxtaposed with the chorus's intricate songs were scenes of intense confrontation, accusation, seduction, and leave-taking played by the actors. All those on stage were men, regardless of the part, dressed in elaborate robes as appropriate to their character and wearing masks.

These masks were not the stiff caricatures that we think of today when we visualize the comic and tragic masks. Rather, the evidence suggests that they were more naturalistic if not individualistic, representing character types. The mask is one of the aspects of Greek theater most foreign to contemporary Western theatrical practice. It is hard for us to think how we could appreciate theater without seeing the details of facial expressions (even more so now when the cinematic close-up enlarges faces to gigantic proportions). But remember that this was a vast, open-air theater and most of the thousands of spectators would have been distant from the scene. It has been argued that the point of the mask was to present the character in the context of a role, not a specific individual, a creature from the distant past, not the present (Taplin: 14). However, at the same time this generality must have clashed with the verbal individuality of the characters (think of Clytemnestra, Electra, Creon, or Helen). In this sense, the mask represented a role that collided with the living language and voice of the actor who spoke the part.

To illustrate the power of Greek tragedy in its own time, we can try to visualize a performance of Euripides' *Bacchae*, a play that is brilliantly self-conscious of its status as theater. *The Bacchae* was Euripides' last play, performed after the poet's death in 404 BCE, when Athens was in the final throes of the Peloponnesian War. It presents the agonizing story of the death of Pentheus, murdered by women – and his own mother – driven mad by Dionysus, who has returned home to Thebes to avenge the city's impiety and make the people believe in his divinity.

The first to speak is the god of theater himself, Dionysus, who enters announcing that the place is Thebes, and that he is a god who has taken on human form to prove that he is a god. The spectators are faced immediately with a paradox: what does it mean to have an *actor* declare that he will convince his audience that he is in fact not what he appears but rather divine and all-powerful? We cannot know exactly what Dionysus' mask looked like, although we can assume that it was as an effeminate man with a curled wig attached, figuring the role that the god played in presenting himself to the others as a priest of Dionysus. The mask must have had a double value: it represented an actor who played a god masked as a human. The mask thus directly challenged the audience's belief in everything it witnessed.

Dionysus is soon joined by the chorus of maenads, ecstatic women who have followed him from Asia, and he gives over the stage to them for their opening choral ode. The audience would have known that these were Athenian men acting as everything they considered to be antithetical to their own nature: women not men, barbaric foreigners not Greeks. This is not the only Greek tragedy in which the chorus is composed of men acting as women, rather than as citizens of the city, but it is the only play that explicitly associates divine power with cross-dressing and acting. In a critical scene, Dionysus enthralls Pentheus, who up to this time has furiously resisted Dionysus' advance into his city and his power over the women of Thebes. Dionysus seduces him into dressing as a maenad himself, so Pentheus can spy on the women celebrating in the hills outside Thebes. The transformation takes place inside the *skene* (the space where the actors changed costumes), and Pentheus emerges from the *skene* in a maenad's garb. Dionysus teaches him literally how to act like a woman, first adjusting his wig and the fit of his gown and then teaching him the maenad's dance step. The message is powerfully ambiguous: the scene brutally mocks Pentheus as he fusses over his wig and robe and spins out his mad fantasies, but it also shows him finally succumbing to the power of Dionysus – and to the power of the theater, embracing the act of transformation required of the male chorus. The transvestite actor is at once abject and divinely possessed.

As he becomes an actor under Dionysus' spell, Pentheus hallucinates, imagining that in looking at Dionysus he sees "two suns / on fire in heaven, and Thebes / double into two cities . . . and you [Dionysus] trot like a bull, with horns sprouting from your head." Dionysus answers triumphantly: "What you see is the god – not hostile, / but helping us, since we've appeased him. / Your eyes see now what they must" (50). But is this the only hallucination in the play? After their first confrontation, Pentheus orders Dionysus to be bound and locked in a stable, and Dionysus is led from the scene. The Chorus then launches into passionate song, calling upon the god for revenge. Then they break into exultation:

> The palace totters, It's going down!
> Look, its front cracks, it's splitting open!
> Dionysus is in there. I feel him!

> Worship him, adore him!
> O I do, I do!
> Watch those columns! They've broken loose from the roof!

Dionysus calls for lightning to strike and burn the palace to the ground and the Chorus calls out again: "Look! Fire blazes up from Semele's tomb" (39). Only then does Dionysus reemerge, still disguised as the priest, celebrating the power of the god "who sent the earthquake rolling through Pentheus' palace."

But what did the audience see in the Theatre of Dionysus? Did the *skene* that represented the palace really crumble to dust? It is not likely. Were the audience meant to be taken in by the illusion or to have a kind of double consciousness that what they *heard* they did not *see*? In his triumphant speech to the Chorus Dionysus relates how he drove Pentheus to think that he was binding the god-priest when he roped a bull:

> Then Bakkhos
> came from nowhere, he rocked the building,
> he blew flames back to life
> on his mother's tomb –
> the palace seemed to catch fire –
> but it burned in *his* mind only. (40)

Is the audience in Pentheus' position, in imagining what the god and Chorus make them imagine? Are we being mocked as well? The central conflict of the tragedy emerges in resistance to the god and the violence of belief, collapsing the world of theater and religious ritual. As Charles Segal asks:

> Is the power of Dionysus, Euripides implicitly asks, something that can hypnotize us, the audience, into thinking that we see something occur that has not in fact occurred (the collapse of the palace) or is it really a means of revealing the presence of divinity among men, or is it both together, that is the power of illusionistic tragedy and of illusionistic (mimetic) art generally to reveal divinity? (220)

Not all Greek tragedy so radically draws our attention to its own staging, but *The Bacchae* reminds us that the conventions of representation on the Greek stage were much more than mere conventions. The mask had the power to bring into relief the contrast and connection between myth and history, that is, between the stylized role associated with the past and the living voice of the actor onstage in the present moment. The convention of the mask, which called upon the audience's capacity to hear and see in different ways, worked with the conventions of the non-illusionistic staging, including the *skene*, the orchestra, and the world imagined beyond, whether the sea or the mountains from which men come mysteriously or to which they go into exile. The bareness of the place and its very openness would have compelled the audience to submit to the force of the language and their own imagination, in order to be able to respond to the actions unfolding before them. Yet it also allowed for a distance from the action, a space for reflection and for a critical response.

English Renaissance Theaters of Illusion

So what did it mean to view a tragedy at Shakespeare's Globe Theatre, if you indeed chose to watch the feigned deaths of men and women rather than the real slaughter of bears and dogs, for your afternoon's entertainment? Like the Theatre of Dionysus, the Globe was open to the soft English sky and the elements, but access to the theater space was also controlled by doors, and one had to pay to get in. As Thomas Platter, a contemporary observer, noted, a man (or woman) may have paid only a penny to enter the theater, "but if he wants to sit, he is let in a further door and there he gives another penny. If he desire to sit on a cushion in the most comfortable place of all, where he not only sees everything well but can also be seen then he gives yet another English penny at another door" (Leacroft: 54). When the spectators took their places, they would face a rectangular platform stage, elevated but still within the reach of those who stood on the ground (as a contemporary drawing of the stage attests; see Illustration 3). The play was almost literally in the groundlings' grasp, and no person, whether on the ground or in the galleries, was probably more than 10 meters away from the action. Those who sat on the stage were part of the spectacle, as well as its witnesses. No matter where the spectators sat or stood, they would have been close enough indeed to ogle the textures of the sumptuous costumes and see the color of the blood.

ILLUSTRATION 3   A contemporary drawing of the Swan Theatre, London, by Thomas Platt. *Photo Bridgeman Art Library*

And what did they see when they came there? Scholars still dispute the layout and the amount of ornamentation of the stage, but we can say with some confidence that the platform stage itself was relatively bare, while basic furniture (a bed, chair, or table) and props (trees, rocks) were brought on and off the stage for scene changes. Philip Henslowe's inventory for the Rose mentions "a tomb, Hell's mouth, a tomb of Dido, mossy banks and a wooden canopy" (Leacroft: 55). A trapdoor in the platform served many purposes, whether as a grave (in *Hamlet*) or access to Hell (as in *Doctor Faustus*). Above the stage a roof jutted out in front of the "tiring house" where the actors readied themselves. Under that roof lay a flat, painted ceiling, called the heavens, which also hid the machinery that allowed some scenic elements to be lowered and raised. In the façade of the tiring house were two doors and an upper gallery, places for musicians to play and for some action (for example, the balcony scene in *Romeo and Juliet*). The space was thus at once barren and evocative, calling upon the imagination and gratifying the eye. The tragic action unfolded between the realms of Heaven and Hell, where the spectators envisioned above, in Hamlet's words, "this brave overhanging firmament, this majestical roof fretted with golden fire," and below, the grave and the habitation of ghosts and devils.

Tragic action in the English Renaissance theater was also action in a way the Greeks would not have recognized it. Whereas Greek tragedy evoked physical violence verbally, the English players made you watch. This was a culture accustomed to witnessing violent spectacle in the course of everyday life, not just in the bear-baiting pits. Public executions, including torture, commonly demonstrated to the public the consequences of crime, and the stage emulated the scaffold in its bloodshed. In an early play, Thomas Preston's *Cambyses*, "a lamentable tragedy mixed full of pleasant mirth," King Cambyses orders Execution to punish a corrupt judge: not only does Execution "smite [the judge] in the neck with a sword to signify this death," but for the delight of the spectators he is also flayed "with a false skin." This infliction of pain went far beyond miming disciplinary punishment. Jacobean tragedy in particular seems to celebrate the extremes of cruelty, including death by poison, strangling, and stabbing.

Unlike the Greeks, who brought their tragedies to one civic space, the early modern English acting companies kept moving, and so they were not confined to acting at the outdoor amphitheaters like the

Globe, Swan, and Rose. In the winter they might be found in indoor spaces like Blackfriars, or they might be called on to perform before the monarch or in the halls of the lawyers at the Inns of Court. They also traveled to inn yards in the provinces, when the plague closed the city theaters and forced the companies on the road. Thus, whereas a play like *The Bacchae* was created for performance in one place and at one time, *Macbeth*, *King Lear*, or *Hamlet* had to work in very different settings – and for potentially very diverse audiences. How, indeed, might the harrowing storm scenes of *King Lear* have played differently on the outdoor stage of the Globe in the sight of apprentices, pick-pockets, merchants, and ladies and gentlemen as opposed to the ornate great hall of Whitehall before King James and his courtiers?

The indoor theaters are sometime referred to as "private theaters," but mostly this means that it cost more to attend performances there and thus the members of the audience were wealthier. These theaters were rectangular rather than polygonal, and the spectators mostly jostled together on benches on the floor or in galleries around the side, while some might be found preening on the stage, ready to be seen as much as to see. Because it was roofed, the playhouse would have been lit by candles, significantly changing the atmosphere to a closer, more stifling environment.

In contrast, when the acting companies took their plays to court upon royal command, the performances took place in ceremonial halls that evoked a sense of royal majesty. The old great hall at Whitehall served for the presentation of plays and masques until Inigo Jones's Banqueting House was completed in 1622 (Mullin: 39). We do not know much about how tragedy was performed at court, and we can only speculate as to how much it made use of the new special effects that were being developed for the elaborate court masques (see Leacroft: 63–6). What we do know is that at all performances at court the most important spectacle was the monarch, even more so than the play, for no one would have sat with his or her back to the king or queen. Any political tragedy performed at court must have been made more poignant by the presence of monarch and courtiers reflecting the royal images enacted before them.

The variety of places of performance for English tragedy reflects its complex roots. Tragic theater did not burst spontaneously forth in London in the final two decades of the sixteenth century. It was cen-turies in the making, in places both sacred and secular. From the twelfth century right up through the sixteenth century people wrote and performed "mystery" or cycle plays, which portrayed biblical events. While the earliest performances appear to have been either in church or at the church door in conjunction with holy days, over the years the venue of mystery plays shifted to city streets and market-places. The plays became the responsibility of the town guilds, who wrote and performed often spectacular episodes on wagons dragged through the town, with citizens playing all the roles, angels or devils, kings or shepherds. The mystery cycles conveyed the message that the events of the Bible and the life of Christ (serious and comic, cosmic and lowly) were very much present in the lives of the citizens, and in the end they also made it clear that theater belonged to the city and to its people and not to the church (see Clopper).

But serious drama was not only happening in the street. It was also to be found in well-to-do households, inn yards, and schools, where either amateurs or groups of traveling professional players put on what we now call "moralities" or moral interludes, short plays that staged a battle between allegorical representations of good and evil for the soul of "Mankind" or "Everyman." The earlier moralities may have been played outdoors, but by the sixteenth century they were primarily private theatrical events, centering on the themes of education, self-control, and moral doctrine considered suitable for the better sort of families or for children and students.

By the end of the sixteenth century, when English tragedy burst into full flower with the plays of Marlowe and Shakespeare, English audiences were thus accustomed to seeing theater live in the midst of their everyday world, whether in the streets or in the quasi-public spaces of their homes and schools. Yet matters changed radically in London, first in 1567 with the building of the Red Lion Theatre in Whitechapel, and then, more significantly, with the construction of the spectacular open-air *Theatre* in Shoreditch in 1576 (Gurr: 13). Built by James Burbage and John Brayne, this new theater, with its polyg-onal structure and open galleries, blazed the way for the later amphi-theaters like the Globe, Rose, and Swan. The creation of this new theater signaled a new freedom for professional playwrights and actors: as Margreta De Grazia puts it, "In 1576, it might be said, the theater became free to occupy its own time and space" (De Grazia 1997: 13). In the theater and its successors, tragedy became disengaged from the world of the church, on the one hand, and the state on the other.

While the acting companies still nominally operated under aristocratic or royal patronage, they were preeminently commercial, thriving on the attendance of all ranks of city folk and flourishing outside the halls of the universities, schools, and aristocratic households that had defined the audiences and themes of the moral interludes. The acting companies were bound by the constraints of censorship, but their commercial orientation also pulled them toward the tastes and desires of their new audience. This new theater was also liberated from any associations with the liturgical year and from any obligation to represent biblical material, while it never entirely lost its connections with a broader sphere of significance.

If *The Bacchae* is the extreme example of a play that exploited the nature of Greek theater, among English Renaissance tragedies, *King Lear* may be the one that most provocatively demonstrates how performance in public vs. private, civic vs. royal, space could shape its meaning. Like *The Bacchae*, *King Lear* strongly calls on the powers of the imagination and challenges our sense of what is real and what is not. It also depicts the downfall of a king, a story that would have resonated differently for common and royal audiences. In *King Lear* an aged king decides to divide his power and revenue among his three daughters and their husbands, while he wishes to retain his authority. He sets up a contest among his daughters as to who can say she loves him most: two perform cynically well, but the third, Cordelia, can say nothing extravagant of her love, in her honesty, and she is banished. Lear then places his fate in the hands of his other two daughters, who systematically rob him of all his dignity. As Lear is stripped of his trappings of authority, he increasing loses his grip on reality. At the play's height, he goes mad in the wilderness, accompanied by a fool and a man who feigns madness, the fugitive Edgar of the subplot. As the play progresses it further blurs the line between reason and madness, reality and fantasy, or most fundamentally, between what is something and what is nothing.

In a performance of *King Lear*, the stage of the Globe Theatre had to stand for many different places: a castle room, a courtyard, a blasted heath in a violent storm, a field at Dover. What the audience would see, literally, with their eyes, would be the familiar platform stage backed by the decorated face of the tiring house, and perhaps a chair, throne, table, or bed to signify an interior scene, or the stocks or a shrub to indicate the outdoors. Darkness, paradoxically, would be signaled by someone bearing a torch or lantern. The audience would have to rely on the actors' words to understand what it was supposed to "see."

However, as the play proceeded and Lear's madness exploded on stage, the audience would have been less able to rely on those words. Lear sees things that the other characters do not, when he raves in the storm on the heath and imagines his daughters are present to be judged, while the feigned madman assents to his visions and only the fool demurs. Later the spectators witness Edgar pretending to lead his blind father, Gloucester, to the edge of a cliff at Dover, trying to convince his father through words alone that he is climbing a steep hill, all so that he can deceive his father into thinking that he has been miraculously saved from his own suicide attempt. By the time that Edgar evokes the climb in words, the audience may at least temporarily not know what to believe. Are Edgar's words the standard theatrical illusion-making of the Renaissance stage, which uses language to transport us to another place, or is it just for Gloucester's benefit, and thus the audience is supposed to know better? The final lines of the play question what we see, when Lear's last words direct our eyes to the body of Cordelia: "Do you see this? Look on her! Look her lips. Look there, look there." What *are* we supposed to see there? And what are we meant to think that Lear sees there? What is the significance of the gap – or conjunction – of the two? At the end, the spectators cannot know what they are supposed to see and think. Perhaps they are meant to pity Lear for his last self-deception, for thinking that Cordelia breathes in the end. But hasn't the audience itself already embraced too many such illusions?

King Lear is a tragedy of knowledge, exposing the fragility of our senses and rational thought, and like *The Bacchae*, it is a tragedy of belief. The persistent theme of sight, omnipresent in the Gloucester–Edgar–Edmund subplot, goes far beyond the illusion and reality cliché. The idea of sight is always intertwined with the concept of "nothing" that recurs so insistently throughout the play. The play seems intent on disproving Lear's initial declaration to Cordelia that "nothing will come of nothing." Partly there is bitter irony in this statement, since terrible consequences come from "nothing" in the play, whether it is Cordelia's pregnant "nothing" or Edmund's "nothing" that it is the forged letter that he uses to entrap Edgar. But Cordelia's love for Lear is also a "nothing" that is a powerful force.

Seeing "something" where there is nothing can be at once destructive and deeply redeeming.

What would have happened with the shifting of the play to the court of King James? We don't know exactly how the scene would have been set at court, but certainly the playing space was very different from the open-air, commercial space of the Globe Theatre associated with common entertainment. Instead the setting would have been a royal palace, a space not unlike the castle hall where *King Lear* begins. As the play progressed that hall would have to melt into a castle courtyard, and then expand even more into the space of the blasted heath and the field at Dover. While the courtiers watched the space increasingly stripped of its royal and even human associations, they would also witness the shrinking of a king's eminence, first in power, then in followers, and finally in clothing, until he became, like Edgar, "unaccommodated man." Remember that the courtly audience saw two kings before them: the one onstage and the other their own king, since everyone was in a position to watch the king watching the play. What would that king have thought of that vision of the torment and degradation of an anointed prince, as he sat there in his own palace, dressed in magnificent robes, bathed in the flattering gazes of his courtiers?

Like Greek tragedy, English Renaissance tragedy was powerfully defined by its limits as well as its capacity for representation. Its productions needed to be mobile, adaptable to a variety of playing spaces and resonant, however differently, in all of them. The intimacy of all these theaters did allow for a use of detail that would not have been possible in the Greek theater, and such details strengthened the connection between actor and audience. At the same time, however, as in the Greek theater, the limitations of staging and the emptiness of the platform stage called upon the spectators to exercise their imaginations. At the beginning of Shakespeare's *Henry V*, the character speaking the prologue asks the pardons of the "gentles" in the audience, for "the flat, unraised spirits that hath dar'd / On this unworthy scaffold to bring forth / So great an object." So, he begs,

> On your imaginary forces work.
> Suppose within the girdle of these walls
> Are now confin'd two mighty monarchies,
> Whose high, upreared, and abutting fronts

The perilous narrow ocean parts asunder.
Piece out our imperfections with your thoughts;
Onto a thousand parts divide one man
And make imaginary puissance. (Prologue, 19–25)

As Shakespeare suggests, the setting created a tension between tragic actor and audience, as to who was ultimately in control of the spectacle and the destiny of its players. But in the end imaginary puissance was a product of both, bound together in a theater of multiple illusions.

French Palaces

The theaters of ancient Athens and early modern England stand as milestones in the history of tragic performance. As performances at Epidaurus in Greece and the recent reconstruction of London's Globe attest, modern audiences are still eager to recapture the experience of attending a play in these theaters. When it comes to French neoclassical tragedy, however, people rarely think of the places where they were played. No one forgets Racine's and Corneille's characters or the weight of their language, but they are unlikely to be able to visualize the stage. But these plays *were* performed, both in public and at court, and the circumstances of their performance shaped the tragedies' expression of confinement and oppression.

The most of famous of these theaters, the home of Racine's tragedies, was the Hôtel de Bourgogne, the theater of the Comédiens du Roi after 1629. (Corneille's plays were performed at the rival Theatre of the Marais.) Originally constructed in 1548 for the Confrères de la Passion and renovated periodically thereafter, the Hôtel was roofed and rectangular in shape, and large enough to hold up to a thousand spectators. While we cannot be exactly sure of all its features, we know that a raised stage at one end faced a parterre or standing-room area. Above the parterre on three sides were rows of cramped loges or seating areas designated for the better sort of spectators. Even with some possible realignment of the loges in the latter part of the seventeenth century, the sightlines must have been awkward. The notoriously disruptive standing-room audience had to look up at the actors' feet, and the audience in the loges either faced each other or craned their necks to see the stage, often from a great distance (see

ILLUSTRATION 4   The crowded space of a seventeenth-century French theater, by Abraham Bosse. *Photo akg-images/Bibliothèque Nationale, Paris*

Illustration 4). Spectators also sat or stood on the stage, where their view must not have been much better (they were also in the habit of disrupting the play by walking around). Like the English indoor theaters, the interior of the Hôtel de Bourgogne was murky, illuminated by candles. The audience might not have been able to see clearly, and so the actors had to rely on their voices and broad gestures to make their points (see Maskall).

This theater that was the unlikely site of such remarkable tragedy was the result of an evolution in which theater moved, as it did in

England, from churches and marketplaces to closed, secular confines. By the mid-sixteenth century, plays in France had lost their direct ties to religion and had become linked to the classical world. The mystery plays were a pan-European phenomenon, in which the high drama of biblical history was played out in the open air or indoors in "mansions" or booths representing different locations. However, as a result of religious conflict in France the mystery plays were suppressed in the middle of the sixteenth century. By the beginning of the seventeenth century, theater artists had begun to argue for new ways of thinking about the stage. In mid-fifteenth-century Italy, scholars, architects, and playwrights had led the way in reconceiving the classical theatrical setting, drawing on the ancient Roman writer Vitruvius' descriptions of Greek and Roman theaters. They took from Vitruvius the form of an amphitheater and the notion that the stage should be backed by a *frons scaena* or scenic façade with doors for exits and entrances. Vitruvius also proposed that there should be three kinds of scenic decoration – tragic, comic, and satiric – where "tragic scenes are delineated with columns, pediments, statues and other objects suited to kings" (Mullin: 8). For a Renaissance audience this design would have associated tragedy with the ruins of the classical world as well as with kings. In the 1530s Sebastiano Serlio reinterpreted Vitruvius to construct a playhouse along classical lines in which an amphitheater faced painted scenery offering a perspective view of Vitruvius' archetypal scenes.

Such Italian concepts did take a long time to make their way north to Paris. They influenced the style of spectacular court theater and opera, but they had little impact at first on the public theaters where classical tragedy developed. French neoclassical tragedy emerged, not in a Vitruvian theater that emanated classical order but rather in the rowdy indoor public theaters of the city of Paris. Unlike the opera houses fitted out with stage machinery for special effects, the playhouses for tragedy and comedy were relatively plain and inflexible in shape, more like the tennis courts (where some had originated) than the opulent halls of court (Maskall: 12).

The design of the French stage space thus evolved over the course of the century, from representing several locations, as on the medieval stage, to representing just one scene, in the classical tradition. In the earlier part of the century, "mansions" would have been juxtaposed with Serlian screen paintings. By the end of the century, both mansions and screens had long given way to a single stage setting, either with painted side wings or a *frons scaena* (Leacroft: 51–2). This simplification corresponded with the dictates of neoclassical dramatic theory, which insisted that the tragic theater represent one action, in one space and one day, to heighten the sense of dramatic truthfulness or what was termed *vraisemblance*. In 1630 Jean Chapelain sent to Pierre Godeau a concise statement of this notion of "true imitation" in theater:

> One of the fundamental principles is that imitation in all works of art must be so perfect that no difference appears between the thing imitated and the thing that is imitating it, for the main source of effectiveness for the representation is to proffer objects to the mind as if they were true and present. (Cited in Goodkin: 384)

The idea was that what the audience saw on stage should be as close as possible to what could be imagined as being performed in that place and that time. Such a sense of *vraisemblance* might only have been heightened when the actors took their plays to court for command performances. Since the tragic action was most often situated in a courtly milieu, and the actors represented nobility in their formal actions and gestures, one might find, as Margaret McGowan puts it, that "what the spectator saw on stage and the evocations to which he responded, constituted a natural extension of his daily experience" (McGowan: 167).

The vagueness of the neoclassical tragic texts about the staging suggests that the scene was simple, against an elaborate painted backdrop. The beginning of Racine's *Iphigénie* announces only that "The scene is at Aulis, in Agamemnon's tent"; for *Phèdre*, "The scene is in Troezen, a town in the Peloponnesus," a designation both very specific and providing almost no information at all. The *Mémoire de Mahelot*, a record of the stage sets used at the Hôtel du Bourgogne in the second half of the seventeenth century, often records the term *palais à volonté* ("palace at will") as instructions to the scene painters to create whatever they wanted to represent a palace (see Maskall: 15–16). What was on stage at the beginning would remain so throughout the play. Beyond the painted backdrop, there was little else to see besides a throne or chair, when required, and doors for entrances and exits. It makes the early modern English stage seem crowded by comparison.

This static nature and constriction of the stage space sent a powerful message: the world of the French neoclassical tragic stage was intense – and suffocating. In his brilliant short study of Racine, Roland Barthes observes:

> Although there is only one setting, according to the rules, one might say there are three tragic sites. There is first of all the Chamber: vestige of the mythic cave, it is the invisible and dreadful place where Power lurks. . . . The Chamber is contiguous to the second tragic site, which is the Antechamber, the eternal space of all subjection, since it here that one waits. The Antechamber (the stage proper) is a medium of transmission; it partakes of both interior and exterior, of Power and Events, of the concealed and the exposed. (3–4)

Barthes's symbolic division of space echoes the design of the palace of the absolute monarch in seventeenth-century France. To gain access to the innermost chamber that was the locus of monarchical power, one had to proceed from antechamber to antechamber, in increasing degrees of hope and fear. Barthes exposes the fact that, while the neoclassical tragic stage may be occupied by princes, it is not itself the locus of power. Rather, it defines a state of exposure and trembling, of not knowing or half-knowing.

In Barthes's taxonomy, the third tragic site is the "Exterior": "The exterior is in fact the site of nontragedy; it contains three kinds of space: that of death, that of escape, that of the event" (5). Like Greek tragedy, French neoclassical tragedy relied a great deal on what was *not* represented on stage. The invisible exterior meant freedom to be sought through escape, an escape usually found only in death (which always took place offstage). In its emphasis on *vraisemblance*, or on showing only what could be realistically imagined to occur in one place and in one time frame, neoclassical tragedy meant to leave nothing to the imagination. In another way, however, it left *everything* to the imagination, in the world beyond the door. Actors and audiences were locked together in the dim, murmuring confines of the theater, bound together through the power of the actors' voices and their bodies.

How would such circumstances of production have shaped the meaning of a play like Racine's *Phèdre*, a tragedy defining a conflict between freedom and oppression, escape and death? In the muted light of the stage, the audience would see an almost empty set. The

Mémoire de Mahelot records that for *Phèdre* the setting was "un palais vouté. Une chaisse pour commence": a vaulted palace painted on the screen and a single chair (Maskall: 112–14). Two characters, young Hippolyte and his mentor, Théramène, would enter, dressed in the fashionable clothing of seventeenth-century Paris. Hippolyte's very first words announce that he will *leave* the scene to join his absent father Thésée: "It is resolved, Théramène, I go" (149). His words thus set up the play's dominant tension emanating from the characters' desire to flee the scene and their own desires, and their inability to do so. Throughout the plays this dynamic is marked by powerfully charged and often unanticipated entrances and exits from the unchanging stage space. Hippolyte is soon pressed from the stage by the impending arrival of his stepmother Phèdre, who is tormented by the need to resist her hidden desire for him. Throughout the play, Hippolyte reenters and then attempts once again to leave, but he cannot really free himself until he is forced from the stage for good by Thésée's order of banishment and his sentence of death. The static stage space thus serves as an emblem of desire that cannot be escaped except through death.

In *Phèdre* what is not staged, or what is hidden from view or unspoken, is ambiguously powerful, reflecting the paradoxes of this theater's conventions of representation. The engine that drives the plot is Phèdre's hidden love for Hippolyte, which changes everything when it finally erupts into speech. The absence of Thésée, offstage until the middle of the play, weighs heavily on all the characters. Phèdre's declaration of love is made possible by the report of Thésée's death, which then makes it all the more shocking when he in fact materializes on the stage. Thésée displaces Hippolyte when he sentences him to his doom and death at the hands of Neptune. The prince is given one last scene of farewell with his beloved Aricie, and he then bolts into the "exterior," which is at once the world of his release and death. But his release occurs at an immense cost to Thésée, who must bear the burden of the sentence he has passed. In Thésée's case, to hold the stage signifies a loss of power and subjection.

The staging of French neoclassical theater thus grants immense significance to the act of representation itself, within the bounds of the stage space that was so powerfully confined. Hippolyte's final "appearance" in the play occurs in Théramène's messenger speech, which records in painful detail Hippolyte's death in a battle with a sea monster in which he falls entangled in the reins of his terrified horses. This speech is the only one in the play that describes a complex physical action and a place, a world existing outside the vaulted palace and the passion and hatred expressed by its characters. It is a speech of remarkable violence, full of blood and water, with Hippolyte's body described as "one whole wound" (211). This is the first and final time that the audience would be released from the scene in front of them in their imaginations. It puts into sharp relief the effect of the performance, which was to fix the audience's mind and eye on what is represented, to the exclusion of everything else. Thomas Lawrenson has observed of the Hôtel de Bourgogne that it "was granted to the least impressive theater edifice of the century, and to it alone, to catch some reflection of the cohesion, the oneness of place, of the ancient theater" (10–11). Unlike the ancient theater, however, this place allowed no view of the sky and city, no breath of air.

The Prison of the Real

Vraisemblance in the French neoclassical theater reached toward a kind of "truth-seeming" in the theater that matched the culture of the time, a sense of truth embedded in the idea and the ideal. But that truth was very different from the real. The "realism" of the neoclassical theater was tied itself to reason, when the spectator was bound to witness onstage what he or she could reasonably apprehend in the time and space allotted.

But this was not real in the way we have come to think of the term today. It was not until the middle of the nineteenth century that what we think of as realistic theater took hold across Europe, that is, a theater in which men and women inhabited stage spaces that replicated the audience's lives. The new school of thought called Naturalism argued that people were shaped by their environment. In well-known words Émile Zola declared the doctrine: "Instead of abstract man I would make a natural man, put him in his proper surroundings, and analyze all the physical and social causes that make him what he is" (151). "Natural man" onstage is a man surrounded by the stuff and form of his life. In Bert States's words, in the new world of stage realism, "the stage picture ceases to be a construct of language, an anywhere between elsewheres, and is now moored to a here and now in which is lodged the very determinism of character and destiny" (45).

Later chapters will consider in more detail what it means to find tragedy in a theater thus rooted in the real. If you agree with George Steiner that tragedy died with the loss of an earlier "ordered and stylized vision of life, with its bent toward allegory and emblematic action" (290–8), you might ask how tragedy could be enacted in a space littered with clocks, teacups, and umbrellas. However, most readers and scholars (and even Steiner) would be willing to accept that Ibsen created a distinctive tragedy of modernity. As such, he did so using the conventions of realistic theater.

By the time that Ibsen brought his new theater to the stage in Europe in the late 1880s, European playhouses had been transformed. A redesign of the seating areas into either a horseshoe or semicircular shape significantly improved the sightlines for most spectators, who would all have faced a stage elegantly framed by a proscenium arch. However, while they might all have had a better view, they would have been more socially stratified, defined by their places. Shakespeare's and Racine's audiences in the public theaters were differentiated by who was sitting and who was standing, where a few extra pennies earned one the right to sit. In the nineteenth-century theaters, the social classes were often strictly divided. Segregated refreshment areas and separate entrances and lounges ensured that no one would have to mix with the lesser classes (Booth: 339).

What they saw on stage, too, would have been very different from what the seventeenth-century spectator witnessed. The proscenium arch defined the stage like a picture frame: "What happened behind it, thanks to the skills of the scene-painter, the gasman, the carpenter and the limelight operator, was thoroughly painterly: the frame proscenium heightened the pictorial nature of acting and production" (Booth: 339). By the latter part of the nineteenth century, in a search for greater realism, stage designers had replaced the old wing and border scenery with a box set that replicated the look of a "real" room with walls and a ceiling (Leacroft: 120). The audience then had the experience of appearing to look through the fourth wall defined by the proscenium frame. The downstage area, where actors had once come close to the audience, disappeared (and it had been a long time since the audience itself was seated on stage). The stage space itself became filled with the trappings of everyday life: furniture, paintings,

ILLUSTRATION 5   A domestic scene from Henrik Ibsen's *A Doll's House*, Royal Theatre of Copenhagen, 1879. *Photo Det Kongelige Bibliothek, Copenhagen*

lights, windows, food, books – anything that was not indecent (States: 41; see also Illustration 5).

Perhaps more than anyone else of his time, Ibsen endowed his plays with a sense of tragedy embedded in the real world. Nineteenth-century audiences might have accepted the intrusion of the stuff of common life into the world of comedy, but it would have seemed antithetical to the grand schemes of tragedy. But by the 1880s Ibsen had come to understand that "this illusion [he] wished to produce was that of reality. . . . My new drama is no tragedy in the ancient acceptation; what I desired to depict were human beings" (1908: 268–9). The human beings he created are inseparable from the material environment that constituted that reality. The things that surround them become both the conditions and symbols that define their existence.

The play that most powerfully demonstrates this effect is *A Doll's House*, where a woman is entrapped in domestic space and defined by objects, yet also stands always on the threshold, poised between the worlds on and off the stage. The text of *A Doll's House* begins with a highly detailed description of the stage setting that offers clues about those comfortable but not yet rich members of the bourgeoisie who are about to inhabit the scene:

> A comfortable room, tastefully but not expensively furnished. A door to the right in the back wall leads to the entryway; another to the left leads to Helmer's study. Between these doors, a piano. Midway in the left-hand wall a door, and farther down a window. Near the window, a round table with an armchair and a small sofa. On the right-hand wall, toward the rear, a door, and nearer the foreground a porcelain stove with two armchairs and a rocking chair beside it. Between the stove and the side door, a small table. Engravings on the wall. An étagère with china figures and other small art objects; a small bookcase with richly bound books; the floor carpeted; a fire burning in the stove. It is a winter day.
>
> A bell rings in the entryway; shortly after we hear the door being unlocked, Nora comes into the room, humming happily to herself; she is wearing street clothes and carries an armload of packages, which she puts down on the table to right. She has left the hall door open; and through it a delivery boy is seen, holding a Christmas tree and a basket, which he gives to the maid who let them in. (43)

The first impression is of a place that is at once attractive yet also confined, furnished with all the elements of domestic life that define the culture of the housewife. Yet from the first minutes of the play, before a word is spoken, as much with French neoclassical tragedy, we can also see the action is defined by a tension between the worlds inside and outside. It begins with Nora's opening and shutting the door from the entryway, which is the space of transition from the controlled interior to the world of the marketplace outside. The inner door to her husband Helmer's study marks off *his* space, which is vaguely frightening and never seen (nibbling from her bag of forbidden macaroons, Nora "steals over and listens at her husband's study door" [43]). At first it might appear to the largely middle-class audience gazing upon a scene so familiar to themselves that this domestic space is a sanctuary, but the play tells another story.

Over the course of the three acts the gradual changes in the stage set so heavily laden with symbolic objects define the progression of the tragedy. The second act begins when Nora's innocence has been shattered, once Helmer's enemy Krogstad has revealed to her that he knows she committed forgery. The stage directions read:

> Same room. In the corner by the piano the Christmas tree now stands stripped of ornament, burned-down candle stubs on its ragged branches. Nora's outdoor clothes lie on the sofa. Nora, alone in the room, moves restlessly about; at last she stops at the sofa and picks up her coat. (72)

The Christmas tree functions as an obvious symbol of disillusionment (literally, dis-illumination). Nora, with her coat in her hand, is positioned on the threshold. The image signals that her relationship to her home has already been destabilized. She hovers anxiously near the mailbox in fear of the arrival of Krogstad's letter to her husband revealing her crime. The mailbox is like the doorway, but it is also like the house that confines her, since only Helmer has the key.

At the beginning of the third act, Nora has already been displaced from the domestic scene:

> Same scene. The table, with chairs around it, has been moved to the center of the room. A lamp on the table is lit. The hall door stands open. Dance music drifts down from the floor above. Mrs. Linde sits at the table, absently paging through a book, trying to read, but apparently unable to focus her thoughts. Once or twice she pauses, tensely listening for a sound at the outer entrance. (94)

"Upstairs," unseen but heard, Nora dances her tarantella and we await the entrance of Krogstad from the world outside. The audience is thus readied for the play's conclusion, where the most significant action is only heard from offstage. After Nora leaves the shocked Helmer, there is a moment of silence, and he is allowed to imagine for a moment that it might not be so: will it be "the greatest miracle," that Nora will not leave? Then is heard, "From below, the sound of door slamming shut." The ending thus leaves neither him nor us with any illusions.

In the last decade of the nineteenth century, Ibsen's audience would have witnessed themselves and their world represented in vivid detail on the stage in a way that endowed the features of that world with extraordinary significance: Rolf Fjelde paints that symbolism in the broadest terms to suggest that Ibsen turned "the contents of the stage itself and all their intricate relationships, into large-scale metaphors for psychological state and spiritual conditions" (xvi). This effect does open up the stifling world of the box stage, where small acts have great meaning. At the same time, however, the audience senses that the actors are still bound by the materiality of the scene they play – and that material also defines who and what they are. In French neoclassical tragedy *vraisemblance* entraps the characters in a "real" defined by what is probable, as well as the decorum of class and gender. In Ibsen's plays, the actors are imprisoned in the reality of a stage world that also stands for much more, unless, like Nora, they can find their way across the threshold.

Theater and Screen

Since the end of the nineteenth century, the proscenium theaters have been broken up, redesigned, and redefined, as actors and directors themselves have sought to escape the confines of the fourth wall and the frame dividing audience and action. They have drawn on the models of the past, including the bare platform stage of the Renaissance theaters and the round amphitheaters of the Greeks, and once again they have stripped away the stuff of real life to leave much to our imaginations. Tragedy has been restaged and reinvented in that space.

In a very different way, film has changed the whole scale of the landscape on which tragedy is played out. As this chapter has suggested, tragedy is defined by the space and time of its performance, and the ways in which it thus engages its audiences' imagination – and their fears and desires. The Athenian audience witnessed action in a place that was both strictly limited and open: the space of the orchestra encircled the action, and the actors and chorus moved in and outside of its circumference. But everything outside that space was visible as far as the eye could see, except for the interior of the *skene* building, the sinister location of private acts. There tragedy was thus defined by the tension between the private and the civic, the invisible and the visible, the divine and human, both staged simultaneously. The Elizabethan arena theaters were more constricted, just as the wooden "O" was closed on all sides, yet still open to the sky. The flat, raised platform of the stage was a canvas for the imagination, here cut off from the world itself, as a reinvented "globe." With the later movement of the European theaters completely indoors, and the stage's retreat behind the proscenium arch, the space for the action became even more confined, and the imagination of the audience became at once more focused and more, perhaps, in terror of what cannot be seen, drawn to the space that lies outside the boundaries of their permitted view.

But while in the theater, the audience can only range outside the limits of the playing space through its imagination, filmed versions of tragic drama immeasurably expand the limits of the literal playing space. Bert States has noted that in the filmed production of plays in the "Ibsen tradition," when the action is limited to conversation,

> the camera, unable to bear too much sameness, becomes restless; like a child, it longs to be outdoors and usually . . . manages to sneak there, to find windows, one might say, in the tight wall of the stage script. What is sacrificed . . . is the tension between the theatrically given, or allowable space and the destinies to be worked out in it. (68–9).

In that sense, the camera allows the audience to relax and sometimes to escape from their confinement altogether. Susan Sontag noted, in contrasting the use of space in film and theater, that theater forces us to see the actors in relationship to each other: when actors are "on" as opposed to off, "they are always visible or visualizable in continuity with each other. In the cinema, no such relationship is necessarily visible or visualizable" (141).

Also, the camera has a resolute habit of filling in for the imagination. In films of *Hamlet*, for example, when Gertrude narrates the watery death of Ophelia, the audience is now allowed to *see* Ophelia's dreamy gathering of flowers and her slipping into the brook. Other cinematic decisions are more controversial. For example, when filming *Macbeth*, directors must decide whether to represent the dagger that Macbeth thinks he sees. "Is that a dagger I see before me?" he asks, and in the theater, the audience members must judge for themselves what he really sees. But in Roman Polanski's film version of *Macbeth*, the audience also sees a spectral dagger hovering before him: we thus incontrovertibly witness his vision, which thus significantly alters the meaning of the scene. The tension between what can be known and what is unknowable through the senses and the imagination can thus collapse in the filming of tragedy, which shows and tells all.

What difference will it make to move the experience of tragedy from live performance to the screen? The camera can indeed go everywhere, places the theater could never show us. But until we live in a world of holograms, it cannot reproduce the three-dimensionality of live theatrical performance (Bentley: 108). Theater involves the presence of people, not their images (although, as André Bazin has argued, those images have their own reality, insofar as "the cinema-like mirror which relays the presence of the person reflected in it . . . is a mirror with a delayed reflection, the tin foil of which retains the image" [112]). It is true that the camera can bring us closer to the actor, and so we may feel more their presence – or the illusion of their presence. While the camera does indeed widen the frame, it also tightens it. The camera, with its capacity to direct our attention to detail and to focus obsessively on facial expression and gesture, invests tragedy in the individual. Ingmar Bergman observed of his own films that "we should realize that the best means of expression the actor has at his command is his look. The close-up, if objectively composed, perfectly directed and played, is the most forcible means at the disposal of the film director" (233). In contrast, in the theaters of Greece, England, and France, the tragic actor's most powerful means of focusing the audience's attention was the live voice and thus the word, not the image. The screen image both enhances and distances the body of the actor, while it displaces the word.

The actors in theater also live in real, linear time, but the screen image can be replayed or re-looped, and the performance is the same every time. Because tragedy is so concerned with time, this makes a difference. As Aristotle and the neoclassical theorists knew, we feel acutely the passage of time in tragic performance, and the closer the elapsed time comes to the "real time" of our experience of it in theater, the more we feel its pressure. Tragedy exercises its power over us because of both the enigma of the future and the absolute nature of the past: once an act has been done before us, it cannot be undone. Film, in contrast, has been more successful in playing with the possibilities that, through a small alteration in events, the outcome could be otherwise. (For example, in Tom Tykwer's *Run Lola Run* [*Lola Rennt*] we are shown three possible scenarios for Lola to save her petty criminal boyfriend from disaster in the process of 20 minutes of elapsed time.) Film in that sense often foregrounds the fact that time is at the heart of the tragic experience, as it tempts us with the dream of escaping time altogether.

The last chapter of this book will return to the question of a future for tragedy if it lives on the screen rather than embodied in action in live theater. While some cultural critics will argue that tragedy as we know it cannot survive in our fragmented world of video clips and sound bites, we must come to terms with the need to reinvent tragedy for that world. For indeed, we still have a profound need for it.

CHAPTER 2

Tragic Form and Language

Woven into the frenzied plot of frustrated love in Shakespeare's *A Midsummer Night's Dream* runs a rehearsal for a tragedy. To celebrate the marriage of King Theseus and his bride Hippolyta, Bottom the weaver and his rustic colleagues practice and perform their play, "The most lamentable comedy and most cruel death of Pyramus and Thisby." And it is indeed a lamentably delightful parody of every convention of tragic performance and language in Shakespeare's time, framed in a story of Pyramus, "a lover that kills himself most gallant for love" (2.2.23–4).

Bottom, who is "set down for Pyramus," protests at first that he would prefer to play a tragic tyrant: "I could play Ercles [Heracles] rarely," he boasts, "or a part to tear a cat in, to make all split," and he recites with pleasure a "lofty" speech in "Ercles' vein." But in the end he condescends to play the lover, while his language is hardly less "splitting." His dying speech is a masterpiece of bathos:

> Come, tears, confound,
> Out, sword, and wound
> The pap of Pyramus;
> Ay, that left pap,
> Where heart doth hop. [Stabs himself.]
> Thus die I, thus, thus, thus.
> Now am I dead,
> Now am I fled;
> My soul is in the sky.
> Tongue, lose thy light,

Moon; take thy flight, [Exit Moonshine.]
Now die, die, die, die, die. [Dies.] (5.1.295–306)

Shakespeare thus pokes fun at the loftiness of tragic language in which he himself so liberally indulged: the flourishes, redundancies, circumlocutions, invocations – and the sheer absurdity of someone's saying so much while he dies.

Even in the tragedies, Shakespeare seems acutely aware of the thin line between high tragic words and nonsense. Hamlet may admire the player's speech about Hecuba's grief, when the player moves himself to tears. Hamlet wonders, "What would he do / Had he the motive and [the cue] for passion / That I have? He would drown the stage with tears, / And cleave the general ear with horrid speech" (3.1.560–3). But when Hamlet himself lets tragic furor fly, he can only go so far: "Why, what an ass am I!" he mocks himself, "This is most brave, / That I, the son of a dear [father] murthered, / Prompted to my revenge by heaven and hell, / Must like a whore unpack my heart with words, / And fall a-cursing like a very drab, / A stallion" (3.1.582–7). In his dying breath, Hamlet knows, in the end, that words must fail him, when "the rest is silence" (5.2.358).

How do you know a tragedy when you see one? Is it in the seriousness of the theme, or the style? Traditionally tragedy has been defined by its formality, so often galling to modern audiences accustomed by film and television to gazing into a perfect mirror of their own casual look and language. But the very first tragedies were deliberately distinct from "real life," and this element that defined them was preserved, even as they were transformed, in the succeeding centuries. This chapter explains the key parts of traditional tragic form, including the chorus, verse, conventions of language, and the controversial unities of time, place, and action, underlining how they function both as artifacts of performance and vehicles of tragic meaning. The conventions of tragic form are not empty rules; rather, they shape the significance and the emotional impact of the art.

Tragic Parts

From the first encounter, it should be immediately clear that a Greek tragedy differs from a modern play. While modern editors and

translators may take pity on the reader and provide some stage directions, the tattered papyri that survive from antiquity mark nothing
but the sequence of speeches: there are no divisions into acts, no cues
for gestures, no indications of emotion. But what looks like an undif-
ferentiated sequence of words is in fact highly structured, the parts
marked out for the reader and the performer through variations in
meter and stanzas.

The parts of Greek tragedy were shared by the actors and the
chorus, the former speaking and the latter singing. This structure
marks tragedy's relationship to older forms of ritual choral song, and
especially the dithyramb, a choral hymn in honor of Dionysus that
was sung by fifty men or boys. Most often, a Greek tragedy will begin
with a prologue spoken by an actor. This persona may be a god,
announcing his or her plans for the play, or perhaps an ordinary figure,
like the lowly watchman at the beginning of *Agamemnon*. (Two older
plays by Aeschylus, *The Persians* and *The Suppliants*, begin with the
procession of the chorus.) Typically the prologue is then followed by
the chorus's entrance song, called the *parodos*. The tragedy then unfolds
through the interplay of the choral odes (the Greek term is *stasimon*,
or *stasima* in the plural) and the scenes of dialogues (or *episodes*). Sometimes the actors engage the chorus, often in common lamentation
(then it is called a *kommos*). The final scene, the *exodos* (which parallels
the *parodos*), can take many forms, but more often it feels less like a
crescendo and more like a sigh.

Using this basic form, Greek tragedians achieved an astonishing
range of dramatic effects. The first play of Aeschylus' *Oresteia*, for
example, begins with a moment of ominous quiet. A watchman lies
alone on the roof waiting, as he has for years, for the beacon that will
signal that Troy is taken and that his king Agamemnon will return
home. His measured, personal words give way to the entrance of the
chorus of old men of Argos, who shift from the intimacy of speech to
the power of song, recalling the history of Argos and the war in strange
images of raptors and fire. With the entrance of Clytemnestra, their
lyric majesty is replaced by a brisk exchange of dialogue between the
queen and the chorus leader. The chorus's baroque vision of the terrible weight of history contrasts with Clytemnestra's directness, energy,
and self-possession. The episode concludes with a second ominous
choral ode, followed by the entry of a herald, who comes to tell of
Agamemnon's imminent return. The next choral ode dwells on the

dangers of human pride, in images dense with myth. Quite fittingly, the triumphant Agamemnon enters, bearing Cassandra as his war prize. In a long speech Agamemnon boasts of annihilating Troy; Clytemnestra then sweeps onstage and counteracts his vaunts with a cunning speech of what appears to be praise but is in fact a seduction to him to enter the house by walking on tapestries, which would be an act of hubris. A tense exchange of *stichomythia* (short lines of counterpoised dialogue) ensues, as Clytemnestra parries every point Agamemnon makes, until he tramples the tapestries and plods to what we know is his certain death. In an interval, the chorus murmur their fears, until Clytemnestra reenters to call Cassandra into the house. Like a wild bird, Cassandra performs a *kommos* with the chorus. She cries out in riddles her vision of the disaster to come, mixing the lyric tone of the chorus with the directness of the spoken word. The last scene of the play is a tortured exchange between first Clytemnestra and the chorus, and then Aegisthus and the chorus, in which the protagonists exult in their act of murder and the chorus reacts in terror. This exchange evokes the structure of the *kommos* while it undercuts it: the chorus laments, but the actors speak in triumph, and the play closes, not with the chorus's sigh of resignation, but with Clytemnestra's assertion of power.

Thus, in *Agamemnon*, as in so much of Greek tragedy, the simple structure of balance between chorus and episodes lends itself to a multitude of emotional and rhetorical effects. The often intense and immediate confrontations of the actors' dialogues may appear to be relieved by the choral odes, but in fact, the choral odes themselves are often filled with a sense of foreboding and emotional charge. They create suspense as much as the action does itself, while they also broaden our perspective on the events taking place, often situating those events in their mythic prehistory. The effect of the play depends on the formal conventions, which structure the audience's expectations and manipulate them to produce both suspense and satisfaction.

Chorus

The structure of Greek tragedy is thus a powerful instrument, capable of manipulating mood, creating tension, and modulating between intense personal action and lyric introspection. Key to that structure is the interplay between actors and chorus. While for some modern readers, the choral odes are just the difficult poetry that you need to plow through before you get to the action, in the greatest tragedies, the choral odes are intrinsic to the action. In any case, as many commentators have pointed out, in its own time the Greek tragic chorus would not have seemed alien, in what John Herington has called a "song culture" (3–5). As Helen Bacon puts it: "music – that is, song, words and dance – was the normal way of giving structure and coherence to utterances of groups like those that participate in Greek tragedy" (11). Looking back, at a distance from such a culture, August Wilhelm Schlegel described the Greek tragic chorus as the ideal, or idealized, spectator, but they are neither "ideal" nor mere bystanders to the action. The chorus exists both in and outside of the action: they participate in the drama at the same time that they comment on it, from the perspectives of both the mythic past and contemporary Athenian values.

The role of the chorus changed over the course of the development of Greek tragedy. It has the strongest presence in the tragedies of Aeschylus. For example, in *The Suppliants*, the chorus itself is the focus of the plot: the fifty daughters of Danaus flee to Argos for protection from a forced marriage, and the story belongs to them. In a later play, *The Eumenides*, the final play of the *Oresteia*, the chorus of hideous Furies is Orestes' collective tormenter. They must be appeased for the crisis to be absolved, and so they are absolutely critical to the action. In Sophocles' plays, the chorus is less involved in the action, but they do play an important part as an interlocutor for the protagonist, offering criticism and questions. In *Antigone*, for example, the chorus constantly shifts its relationship to both Creon and Antigone. They appear to be afraid of both antagonists, wary of Antigone's extremism but also concerned over speaking out in the face of Creon's anger. They do intervene at a critical point in Creon's life, when he asks them for advice about what to do when confronting Tiresias' threats of doom. At this point they are far from mere commentators on the action. In *Oedipus the King*, in contrast, the chorus comes first as suppliants to the king, but for the most part they are helpless and horrified witnesses of Oedipus' self-destruction. They try, as we do, to make sense of what transpires before them, clearly frightened by the threat they see to everything that grounds the order of the city and man.

In his brief comments on the role of the chorus, Aristotle observes that "the chorus also should be thought of as one of the actors; it should be a part of the whole and contribute its share to success in the competitive effort in the manner of Sophocles, not Euripides" (51, 1456a25–30). Aristotle signals here what was evident in his own time: the gradual attenuation of the chorus's role throughout the classical period. In many but not all of the plays of Euripides, they were indeed reduced largely to bystanders, with some notable exceptions. In *Ion* they play a role in the plot, and in *The Bacchae*, they are relentless advocates for the god and embody the essence of Dionysus' power. But with Euripides' increasing turn toward greater realism in the majority of his plays, the chorus necessarily takes a lesser and more separate role. (For further discussion of the chorus see Calame; also Gould and Goldhill.)

In reinventing tragedy, later writers would try to resuscitate the chorus, but with mixed results, except, perhaps, in the translation of tragedy to opera, which restored the tragic effects of music and choral song. Lucius Annaeus Seneca's re-creations of Greek tragedy look at first glance like their Greek counterparts, but there the choral odes merely mark the divisions between episodes, in effect creating a structure divided into "acts" (see Braden: 35). In Renaissance tragedies an actor called the "chorus" might step out to introduce or comment on the plot, but this figure lives in the world of the audience and not in the world of the play. T. S. Eliot reintroduced the chorus into *Murder in the Cathedral* with great success because of its ecclesiastical setting, but when it came to his *The Family Reunion* critics mocked the ghostly chorus of the Furies, lingering oddly outside the window of the English drawing room where the action takes place. The demands of realism inevitably exclude the corporate presence of the chorus. Its collectivity is at odds with realism's focus on individual characters and its role as a mirror of everyday life. Further, the chorus's implied distance from the action has the power to break the illusion of the mirror.

Unities of Time, Place, and Action

While the tragic chorus now seems particularly archaic, equally puzzling to modern readers are the old disputes over tragic form, and in particular, the "rules" of representation. You can blame Aristotle if you like, but you should really blame those critics who converted

Aristotle's stray observations about Greek theater into prescriptions for writing the ideal tragedy. The Renaissance and eighteenth-century arguments over the form of the perfect tragedy may seem like avoidance of talking about what really matters, but those cultures' concern with verisimilitude, probability, and control was an understandable response to the chaos at the heart of tragic experience.

What is a tragedy, for Aristotle?

> Tragedy, then, is a process of imitating an action which has serious implications, is complete, and possesses magnitude; by means of language which has been made sensuously attractive . . . ; enacted by the persons themselves and not presented through narrative; through a course of pity and fear completing the purification of tragic acts which have those emotional characteristics. (25, 1449b20–30)

Aristotle thus first gives attention to the formal qualities of tragedy, later divided into six parts, which are "plot, characters, verbal expression, thought, visual adornment [or spectacle], and song composition." Aristotle wants to fix what makes a tragedy *beautiful*. What is beautiful is what is "believable," even though what is represented may be horrific. The well-made play has a beginning, middle, and end, or a sense of proportion. Proportion means preferring that the tragedy represent one action in a short time span (30–2, 1450b30–1451a38), or (notoriously) "as far as its length is concerned tragedy tries as hard as it can to exist during a single daylight period, or to vary but little, while the epic is not limited in its time" (24, 1449b10).

Renaissance commentators laboriously extracted from the *Poetics* a theory of what tragedy *should* be. The first Latin translation of the Renaissance appeared in Italy in 1498, but the work of converting Aristotle's musings on tragedy into rules started seriously in 1549 with the appearance of Bernardo Segni's Italian translation, followed by the commentaries of Francesco Robortello (1548), Julius Caesar Scaliger (1561), and Lodovico Castelvetro (1570). These scholars sought to constrict the representation of tragic action to as little as 12 hours, believing it close enough to the time span of viewing the play; and they stipulated that plot and action should be confined to a single place and set of circumstances. From Italy, what thus became the three unities of time, place, and action spread north to France and England.

In England, however, these neoclassical strictures never really took hold. In the 1580s Sir Philip Sidney castigated his countrymen for their tragedies that are "defectious in the circumstances." He complains that even Sackville and Norton's otherwise admirable *Gorboduc* was "faulty both in place and time, the two necessary companions of all corporal actions. For where the stage should always represent but one place, and the uttermost time presupposed in it should be, both by Aristotle's precept and common reason, but one day, there is both many days, and many places, inartificially imagined" (110). How can we ask the spectators to believe the stage is Asia one minute, and Africa another, Sidney wonders, rather disingenuously. Paradoxically, Sidney's lack of trust in the power of the spectator's imagination is matched by his belief in the power of the poet to invent. Thinking he should be asked, "How then shall we set forth a story, which containeth both many places and many times?" Sidney replies with a question: "And do they not know that a tragedy is tied to the laws of Poesy, and not of History; not bound to follow the story, but, having liberty, either to feign a quite new matter, or to frame the history to the most tragical conveniency?" (111). The solution to the paradox lies in the fact that poets can do whatever they like with stories, compressing them into a new time and space, and binding the spectator with the elastic of the imagination.

Sidney was not to win this argument for the unities of time, place, and action so crucial to tragic theory. Most English experiments with neoclassical tragedy were confined to the schoolhouse or manuscript, and when they did reach the popular stage, audiences were not amused. In the preface to his tragedy *Sejanus* (1603), Ben Jonson notes proudly his observing "truth of argument, dignity of persons, gravity and height of elocution, fullness and frequency of sentence" (104) in his sober Roman tale, yet he confesses he neglected the observation of the "strict laws of time" and omitted a chorus, only because his audience would not stand for it (103). In his preface to *The White Devil* (ca. 1612) John Webster acknowledges that his play is "no true dramatic poem," but he also blames his audience:

> For should a man present to such an auditory the most sententious tragedy that ever was written, observing all the critical laws, as height of style, and gravity of person; enrich it with the sententious chorus, and as it were liken death in the passionate and weighty Nuntius: yet, after all this divine rapture, . . . the breath that comes from the uncapable multitude is able to poison it. (7)

Shakespeare, in contrast, never apologized for the fact that Shakespearean tragedy knows few bounds of time or place. In its most compressed form the action might be confined to the walls of a city and its surrounding countryside like *Julius Caesar*'s Rome, or a castle like that of *Hamlet*'s Elsinore, but in its most expansive form, Shakespearean tragedy spans continents and decades, as it does in *Antony and Cleopatra*.

The situation was quite different in France, where the strict literary theory of tragic form that was stillborn in England and Spain flourished. Of course, France has what England never had: the Académie française, founded by Cardinal Richelieu in 1635 as an arbiter of taste and literary practice. French scholars had known about the Aristotelian commentaries, but it was Jean Chapelain who argued for taking theory into practice on stage. Then, on commission from Cardinal Richelieu, the Abbé d'Aubignac wrote a massive book, *La Pratique du théâtre* (begun in the 1640s and finally published in 1657). In this book he outlines all the rules for "regular drama," including the unities of time, place, and action, and strict adherence to decorum. For d'Aubignac and others, the neoclassical rules were not merely ancient dicta. Rather, d'Aubignac declared: "I say that the rules of the theatre are not founded in authority but in reason. They are not established by example but on natural judgment" (66: my translation). We have seen the importance of this appeal to natural reason, or *vraisemblance*, on the neoclassical stage, whereby what is represented should resemble an idealized version of the "real" (see pp. 20–1 above); the unities framed the architecture of *vraisemblance*.

At this moment in history, while these constraints might have proved a halter, they fashioned a crucible for astonishing art. As Timothy Reiss has argued, the moment was perfect, when the rules of tragedy embodied the beliefs of a world as shaped by absolutism and science (chs 9–11). The significance of the unities was played out before the public eye in the controversy over Pierre Corneille's popular play *Le Cid* (1636), which enraged members of the Académie for its violation of the rules. After that, rather than continuing to rebel, Corneille produced three remarkable "regular" tragedies, *Horace* (1640), *Cinna* (1641), and *Polyeucte* (1643). These plays proved incontrovertibly that the rules could produce powerful drama and express the ethos of an age. Jean Racine is the playwright most celebrated for his ability to not just work within the restrictions of the unities, but to use them to maximum effect to create a theater of oppression and urgency. Most notable are *Andromaque* (1667), a tale of frustrated love and hate set after the end of the Trojan War; two tragedies on Roman themes, *Britannicus* (1669) and *Bérénice* (1670); and then the masterful adaptations of Greek tragedy, *Iphigénie* (1674) and *Phèdre* (1677).

But the nervous vigor that sustained the neoclassical tragedies of the time of Louis XIV did not last. In France, neoclassicism eventually gave way to a new romantic temper. At first the spectacle of melodrama seized the French stage, although neoclassicism continued to define the taste of serious drama for quite some time. As the tradition began to collapse under its own weight, it was broken by the revolt led self-consciously by Victor Hugo. In the 1827 Preface to *Cromwell* (a play that was never produced), Hugo mockingly pronounced the death of the unities:

> Why administer the same dose of time to every kind of event? Why use the same measuring instrument in all cases? We'd laugh at a cobbler who wanted to put the same size of shoe on everyone's feet. If we cross the unity of time and the unity of place like the bars of a cage, and bring pedantically into it (courtesy of Aristotle) all the deeds, nations and individuals that Providence lavishes on a vast scale in reality, we'll mutilate people and facts, and make history wince. To go further the whole thing will die on the operating table. That's why the doctrinaire mutilators usually achieve the results they do: everything that was alive in the history books is dead on the tragic stage. And that's why, in most cases, the cage of the unities encloses only a skeleton. (2004: 38)

While the "old ways" were already dying, Hugo's diatribe and his own practice in spectacular plays such as *Hernani* made it clear there was no going back for tragedy. In Germany, Johann Christoph Gottsched tried to introduce neoclassical formal rules to German culture in the early eighteenth century though his *Versuch einer kritischen Dichtkunst für die Deutschen* ("Essay on a German Critical Poetic Theory"; 1730), but in the end, he was less influential through what he said than through the reaction he catalyzed: the creation of a new German national drama that imitated Shakespeare rather than Racine.

Even with the failure of the unities to dominate the tragic form, we should still remember what Aristotle meant from the beginning: there is a difference between the storytelling of epic and tragedy. Epic takes its time to play out a sequence of events when it embraces the sweep of history. Tragedy, in contrast, gains much of its power from its relentless focus on a critical moment in time, what in Greek is called a *kairos*, both a crisis and a test. Epic also does not confine itself to a particular place: it can cross the seas or traverse a continent. Tragedy, however, commonly gains from compression into one castle, one city, even one drawing room, which brings the actors into collision with one another, heightening the intensity of emotion and pain.

The value of this compression of time and space might first seem to have been lost in modern tragic theater. However, one could argue that it survived in the post-realist and absurdist theaters of modernism. Samuel Beckett's *Waiting for Godot* is an extreme example of a play that could be said to exemplify Aristotle's ideas about a beautiful tragedy: that is, as a play that must represent what happens in a strictly limited time that is also timeless and a single space that is everywhere. In this play, two tramps, Vladimir and Estragon (otherwise known as Didi and Gogo), famously do nothing, but talk, fidget, fight, play with hats, and embrace while they wait for Godot, who never comes. The only significant events are the two appearances of Pozzo and Lucky, master and servant bound together by a rope, and by a bond of interminable infliction of pain. One could say that they are two characters in search of a plot (in contrast to Pirandello's *Six Characters in Search of an Author*).

Waiting for Godot has almost a formal, stark simplicity in its action: what you see is what you get, performed in "real time," as it were. Didi and Gogo talk, Pozzo and Lucky enter and depart, in the first act, and the same action is repeated in the second act. The action is perfectly congruent with the time in which it is represented – and indeed, Didi and Gogo worry immensely about the matter of time.

The action is clearly performed in one place, identified by the tree and the mound, and Gogo's boots. In the first act we meet Gogo putting on his boots, sitting on a low mound. In the second act the stage directions tell us that we see "Estragon's boots front center, heels together, toes splayed: Lucky's hat in the same place. The tree has four or five leaves" (62). Like the space of French neoclassical tragedy, the place is *oppressively* the same: the actors do not seem to be able to move from the stage space, being inescapably bound by it.

Further, what is represented in *Waiting for Godot* in that time and place is "believable" or probable. No miracles happen on the stage (except perhaps the incident with Lucky's hat) and the audience is not expected to make a great leap of imagination to grasp what they see before them (as they are, for example, in Shakespeare's *Antony and Cleopatra*, where they are asked to imagine the stage space as being Rome in one moment, and Egypt in the next). What you see is what you get, except for what you don't see, which, as in Greek tragedy, is always represented beyond the grasp of the actors, always offstage. This is the place inhabited by Godot.

But why does it matter? If, as some critics have claimed, Beckett's play is an allegory, it is also painfully realistic in its representation of everyday action in time. But it has the kind of realism that we associate with tragedy in the classical tradition. It is not the realism of a playwright like Ibsen, where the stage is a reflection of the bourgeois living room, stuffed with the things of our everyday lives. Instead, *Waiting for Godot* translates the facts of our lives into universals of time and space. As Aristotle tells us, this is also what distinguishes tragedy from history, "for poetry speaks more of universals [*katholou*], history of particulars [*kath'hekaston*]" (33, 1451b5). As a tragedy in the classical mode, this play is our story, in the same way that Antigone's or Oedipus' can be.

Tragic Verse

Today's popular culture is saturated with verse. Even though we may not recognize it, verse in the form of rock lyrics, rap, and advertising jingles penetrates our headphones and bounces across our televisions and computer monitors on a daily basis. At the same time, however, we fully expect plays to be in prose. In ancient and Renaissance tragedy, however, the use of verse reminds us that tragic discourse is not real in the sense that a conversation at the breakfast table or by the office water cooler is real. We cannot forget that the world of tragedy is both distant and very much with us.

Even if Greek tragedy did indeed originate in song, its emotional power emerges through the interplay of song and speech. The dominant meter of the actors' dialogue is iambic trimeter (six iambic feet), a rhythm that balances short and long syllables (as opposed to stressed and unstressed syllables, as in English poetry). This meter approximated the rhythm of Greek everyday language, or so Aristotle tells us, when he observes that the iambic is "the most speech-like of verses.

An indication of this is that we speak more iambics than any other kind of verse in our conversation with each other, whereas we utter hexameters rarely, and when we do we abandon the characteristic tone-pattern of ordinary speech" (23, 1449a15–30). In contrast, for its entrances and exits, the Greek chorus uses the marching anapaest, the stately meter of procession (Herington: 120–1). Most complex was the metrical form of the choral lyrics, often exquisite patterns in parallel stanzas (the *strophe* and *antistrophe*) followed by a summary *epode*. Each meter seems to have been intended to evoke a distinct feeling: for example, the dochmiac was apparently associated with out-of-control emotions (Herington: 113–44).

Not only did metrical variation produce this intricate music, but the alternation of the actors' iambic dialogues and the chorus's lyric odes also served to contrast present discourse with poetry evocative of the distant past. Jean-Pierre Vernant and Pierre Vidal-Naquet have observed the paradox that while the content of the chorus's songs often expresses contemporary values, their song connects them to the past. Similarly, "even as the setting and the mask confer upon the tragic protagonist the magnified dimensions of one of the exceptional beings that are the object of a cult in the city, the language used brings him closer to the ordinary man" (34). The style of the verse carries more than an emotional resonance: it is also part of the texture of conflicting values and meanings.

In comparison with Greek tragedy, English Renaissance tragedy may appear ungainly and unstructured, but in fact, it is poetry too. But these playwrights knew how to artfully intermix poetry with prose. The dominant form of English Renaissance tragedy is blank verse, or unrhymed iambic pentameter, introduced by the Earl of Surrey in his 1540 translation of Virgil's *Aeneid*, and first used in drama in Thomas Sackville and Thomas Norton's *Gorboduc* (1561). The first tragedy to be composed fully in blank verse was Thomas Hughes's *The Misfortunes of Arthur* (1588), but Christopher Marlowe gets the credit for having fashioned blank verse into a fit vehicle for tragedy. The prologue of Marlowe's *Tamburlaine* (1587) announces his abandonment of "jigging veins of rhyming mother-wits" (105, Prologue.1), his term for his predecessors in tragic composition. Here the author declares that instead you "shall hear the Scythian Tamburlaine / Threatening the world with high astounding terms" (105, Prologue.4–5). Witness, for example, the headlong drive of what Ben Jonson called

Marlowe's mighty line when Tamburlaine woos Theridamas into joining his cause:

> Forsake thy king, and do but join with me,
> And we will triumph over all the world.
> I hold the Fates bound fast in iron chains,
> And with my hand turn Fortune's wheel about;
> And sooner shall the sun fall from his sphere
> Than Tamburlaine be slain or overcome. (1.2.172–7)

While he rarely abandoned the discipline of the end-stopped line, Marlowe also knew how to go against its grain, playing off its measure and authority. For example, the stunning final speech of *Doctor Faustus* is stretched with broken lines and strained caesurae:

> O soul, be changed into little water drops
> And fall into the ocean, ne'er be found!
> My God, my God, look not so fierce on me!
> Adders and serpents, let me breathe a while!
> Ugly hell, gape not! Come not, Lucifer!
> I'll burn my books! Ah, Mephistopheles! (5.2.111–16)

In these last words Marlowe thus expresses Faustus's final agony, his inability to breathe, and his fear of God and time, by working against the pressure of the iamb's march.

In his *Groatsworth of Wit* (1592), Shakespeare's theatrical colleague Robert Greene alluded nastily to Shakespeare as an exaggerated stylist, noting disdainfully that "there is an upstart Crow, beautified with our feathers, that with his *Tygers hart wrapt in a Players hyde*, supposes he is as well able to bombast out a blanke verse as the best of you" (84–5; italics in the original). But of course, Shakespeare was better than all the rest, a master of the form. Further, even more so than any other playwright of his time, he knew how to manipulate the modulations of tragic poetry and prose. The early tragedies include little prose, but over the course of his career he integrated it to great effect, while the change from poetry to prose is not as predictable as the modulations between lyric and iambic trimeter in Greek tragedy. It is not necessarily true, for example, that upper-class characters always speak in verse. For example, Hamlet speaks prose as easily as he does poetry. In his scenes with the players, they speak high verse, while Hamlet speaks urgent prose, contrasting their overwrought aesthetic version of tragedy with his own bitter experience. After the "To be or not to be" soliloquy, Hamlet's encounter with Ophelia is in prose, but his language is no less eloquent, even while unmeasured (see McDonald: ch. 6). Similarly, one can find the more common characters finding a voice in poetry: Enobarbus in *Antony and Cleopatra* may be a rough soldier, but it is he who is given the extraordinary speech describing Cleopatra's' first encounter with Antony on her barge at Cydnus.

The amazing formal flexibility of English Renaissance tragedy contrasts with the strict music of French neoclassical theater composed of rhymed couplets of iambic hexameter (called an alexandrine). No one could mistake this rhythm for speech: Roland Barthes chides contemporary performers for trying "to make the alexandrine into a *natural* language, either by making it prosaic or, conversely, by making it musical. But the truth of the alexandrine is neither to destroy nor to purify itself: it is in its distance" (145). At its best, the rhymed alexandrine is a powerful vehicle of restraint and counterpoint. See, for example, Phèdre's confession of her passion for Hippolyte:

> Je le vis, je rougis, je pâlis à sa vue;
> Un trouble s'éleva dans mon âme éperdue;
> Mes yeux ne voyaient plus, je ne pouvais parler;
> Je sentis tout mon corps et transir et brûler . . .
> (I saw him, I blushed, I grew pale at the sight;
> Trouble rose in my lost soul
> My eyes saw no more, I could not speak
> I felt all my body freeze and burn . . .) (273–6)

The diction here is artfully arrayed in opposites (freezing/burning, pale/red), and the lines push against caesura. The rhyme creates closure while pairing concepts (parler/brûler, vue/perdue). Of course, Racine also knew how to strain the line's structure with enjambment and breaking it into two (see Maskall: 126–9). When Panope exclaims at Phèdre's death, "Elle expire, seigneur!" ("She dies, my lord"), Thésée immediately completes her sentence: "D'une action si noire / Que ne peut avec elle expire la mémoire" ("of an action so dark / That the memory cannot die with her") (1644–6). The line is broken with her death, and the enjambment of Thésée's bitter addition evokes the overflow of the act (even as "noire" neatly rhymes with "mémoire").

In Shakespearean tragedy the rhymed couplet is often used for closure, but such rhymes in French neoclassical tragedy are as essential to the feeling of oppression as are the confines of the stage itself.

In his revolutionary Preface to *Cromwell*, where he rejects the unities, Hugo also calls for a new kind of verse for drama:

> Supposing I had the right to state what style should be used for drama, I'd choose a free, straightforward, faithful kind of verse that dared to say everything without prudery or affectation; a kind of verse that moved naturally between comedy and tragedy, sublimity and grotesquerie; down-to-earth and poetic in turn, always artistic and inspired, profound and startling, broad and true. (2004: 50)

While Hugo himself was not ready to abandon poetry entirely (though he did so with *Lucrezia Borgia*), he hoped to write dramatic poetry as good as prose, that is, as unfettered as possible within the constraints of the alexandrine. Other writers of Romantic tragedy experimented more with the stylistic freedom of prose (for example, Friedrich Schiller in *The Robbers*). But Ibsen was the playwright who most radically staked his claim on the decision to write in prose rather than verse. Tragedy in Ibsen inheres as much in common language as it does in common things.

Later both W. B. Yeats and T. S. Eliot attempted to revive the power of verse drama. Yeats, in particular, wanted to restore tragedy to what he saw as its ritual roots (influenced by what he knew of Nietzsche's theories of tragedy). In plays like *On Baile's Strand* (1904) and *The Only Jealousy of Emer* (1919), Yeats reached back to ancient Irish legends and re-created them in heroic poetry. Eliot's most notable theatrical success was his verse tragedy of Thomas Becket, in *Murder in the Cathedral* (1935), a work which takes place in a hieratic, medieval setting that lent itself to the seriousness of poetry. But as Ibsen sensed, tragedy in modernity effectively demands prose to be present in our lives.

Tragic Language

From its origins, tragedy was both linked to and separated from everyday life, not only by its unique music but also by the quality of its language. Shakespeare's Bottom thought that tragic language was

"Ercles' vein," but tragic eloquence can be simple as well as grand. Aristotle sought to pinpoint the particular quality of Greek tragic language as what was "clear without being low" (58–9, 1458a17–20), if what is "low" is common, or ordinary speech. He argues that the writer can avoid being low by using "alien" terms such as foreign words, dialectic, and metaphors. However, he thought that the writer should not use too much of these devices, because then he would fall into "barbarism." So then, according to the *Poetics*, "foreign words, metaphor, ornamental words, and all other varieties, will ensure that it is not commonplace or low, and the common element will ensure clarity" (59, 1458a30–1458b1). According to this careful formulation tragic language must seem strange while still comprehensible. We must understand it yet also feel somehow in awe or even afraid of it.

Aristotle's effort to steer a path between clarity and height suggests that even in antiquity, tragic style was difficult to define. If you need more evidence of this difficulty, just look at Aristophanes' comedy *The Frogs* and the hilarious and very technical contest between Euripides and Aeschylus, staged to impress Dionysus as to who is the best poet to save the city of Athens. Euripides accuses Aeschylus of being overly obscure: he protests, "Not one word you could understand . . . but battles of Skamandros, barbicans with ditches underneath, / and hooknosed eagles bronze-enwrought on shields, verse armed like infantry, / not altogether easy to make out the sense" (60). In contrast, Euripides boasts of having put tragedy on a diet to ease its "gas pains": "*I* made the drama *democratic* . . . Then I taught natural conversational dialogue . . . I staged the life of everyday, the way we live" (61–2; italics in the original). Aeschylus does not back down at Euripides' claim that "you ought to make people talk like people." Rather, Aeschylus argues, "Your folksy style's for the birds. / For magnificent thoughts and magnificent fancies, we must have magnificent words" (68).

This contest defines the terms for all future debates about what is the most effective language for tragedy: a grand language that stirs the soul and the imagination, or a language that cuts to the bone of how we live and speak in our own lives. John Herington bemoans the fact that we can never truly translate Greek tragedy, for "what we cannot do is to reproduce a dialect which embodied and evoked an entire national poetic tradition, a dialect which was never spoken outside the theatre but was mostly as remote from the language of the streets as the tragic masks and costumes were from the dress of the streets" (127). But sometimes the most powerful lines of Aeschylus are also the simplest ones. At a critical moment in *The Libation Bearers*, as Clytemnestra begs elaborately for mercy, calling on Orestes' memory of the breast he used to suck, Orestes turns to his companion Pylades with a direct question: *"Puladē, ti drasō? Mēter aidesthō ktanein?"* ("Pylades, what do I do? Be shamed to kill my mother?") (see Silk: 467). At moments of crisis, a single word may express the greatest pain.

Even when it appears simple, tragic language radiates ominous power. A single word like Cordelia's "nothing" can set off a fatal chain reaction. Tragic language is often deliberately not transparent, but rather loaded with dark and double meanings. In the *Oresteia*, for example, almost every word that Clytemnestra says could mean something else. Language in that play is divided against itself and full of omens of the coming disaster. The first two plays of the trilogy suggest the power of language to affect events in the ways that omens do. Just as the trilogy as a whole drives to convert blood guilt to law, savagery to civilization, it also works to contain language, bridling its energy to serve social and secular ends (see Peradotto).

Changes in style in the course of a tragedy can also suggest a character's transformation. In *King Lear*, for example, the protagonist knows only one mode of speaking in the first two acts of the play: command and abuse. This style reaches its height in the first moment of Lear's madness, when he confronts the elements in the storm ´on the heath:

> Blow, winds, and crack your cheeks! rage, blow!
> You cataracts and hurricanoes, spout
> Till you have drench'd our steeples, [drown'd] the cocks!
> You sulph'rous and thought-executing fires,
> Vaunt-couriers of oak-cleaving thunderbolts,
> Singe my white head! And thou, all-shaking thunder,
> Strike flat the thick rotundity o' th' world!
> Crack nature's moulds, all germains spill at once
> That makes ingrateful man! (3.2.1–9)

As Aristotle would put it, in the context of the everyday language of Shakespeare's London, this speech is full of "alien" or Latinate words (such as "rotundity," "germains," "sulph'rous"), which make Lear appear both "high" and distant. This speech is also marked by the imperative mood, breaking under its own weight of rage.

Yet it is in this scene of absolute waste, where civilization slips away, that Lear's language starts to change, as his wits "turn." Struck by the hostility and seeing the Fool before him, Lear falls into Anglo-Saxon monosyllables:

> Come on, my boy. How dost, my boy? Art cold?
> I am cold myself. Where is this straw, my fellow?
> The art of our necessities is strange
> And can make vile things precious. (3.2.68–70)

This is the language of our necessities: not "vile" perhaps, but certainly low. It is a moment of pure clarity for Lear, even as he descends into madness.

The language of Lear's madness is always lucid in its elements, if not in its continuities. In his last speech in the play there are only three words longer than one syllable: "undo," "button," and the heavy, repeated "never":

> And my poor fool is hang'd! No, no, no life!
> Why should a dog, a horse, a rat, have life,
> And thou no breath at all? Thou'lt come no more,
> Never, never, never, never, never.
> Pray you undo this button. Thank you, sir.
> Do you see this? Look on her! Look her lips,
> Look there, look there! *He dies.* (5.3.306–12)

The Lear who began with a question – "Who loves me most?" – also ends with the most fundamental of questions, in the most basic language. So the Lear of the imperative mood survives until the end, but the last lines are both a prayer and a command.

Both the "low" and the "high" have thus always been a part of the language of tragedy, for in tragedy words are understood both as a shield from the truth as well as the means to it. Adrian Poole has written eloquently of the effects of silence in tragedy: as he says, "silence can be beautiful, blissful, heroic, agonized, crushing. It all depends whose and when. It also depends on the words and sounds, desired and feared, that we might hear or utter and don't" (82).

Catastrophes occur when a character fails to speak, and sometimes silence or an inarticulate scream may be the only conceivable response to intense pain. Perhaps one of the most moving "speeches" in tragedy is the defiant drumming of the mute Katrina in Bertolt Brecht's *Mother Courage and her Children*, when she drums wildly on the roof to warn the people of Halle of the coming invasion. Shots still her and her drums, but she and they have spoken eloquently. Tragedy also recognizes the failures of language itself, as it teaches us to go beyond speech to where, as Hamlet says, "the rest is silence."

CHAPTER 3

Tragic Plots

The renowned translator and poet Robert Fagles used to begin his tragedy course with a Cold-War-era joke. As Fagles told it, a Soviet professor of literature is endeavoring to explain the genre of tragedy to his baffled students. "What," he asks dramatically, "is tragedy?" A confident student declares: "A car with two young lovers, just married, skids off the road on an icy winter night, and the newlyweds are killed." "No," says the professor, "that is not tragedy: it is a terrible accident, but it is not tragedy. What is tragedy?" A hand starts up, again, and another eager student pronounces: "A huge airliner, full to capacity, suffers engine failure and plunges into the ocean: all aboard are killed." "No," responds the professor, "that is not tragedy: it is a great loss, but it is not tragedy. *What* is tragedy?" There is a silence, and then, from the back of the room, a voice offers: "Rebels attack the Kremlin, set off a bomb, and the entire Commissariat is killed." "Yes, yes," exclaims the professor in wonderment, "*that* is tragedy! But how did you know?" "It's simple," replies the student, "it's no accident; it's no great loss."

The stumbling students in Fagles's story illustrate the anxiety we all face when we try to sort out what constitutes tragedy in a world in which we witness everyday disasters in newspapers, on television, or on the internet. We wonder, then, what makes a tragedy different from all these all too common horrors of life. Aristotle's *Poetics* has a deceptively easy answer for us, which is that *plot* is the essence of tragedy. No amount of somber language, compelling character, or spectacular events can make up for the lack of a plot. So Aristotle is very dismissive of episodic plots, in which it appears that occurrences come about by chance (35, 1451b30–1452a5). Aristotle likens the situation to painting: "the most beautiful pigments smeared on at random will not give as much pleasure as a black-and-white outline picture," and so in a tragedy, the structure of the plot is everything (28, 1450b3). Of course, Aristotle could not have imagined a culture in which random smears of paint would become a kind of art, as it did in the twentieth century. He saw form as essential to tragedy's emotional and aesthetic impact. Now that the relationship between form and art has been exploded, has the force of the tragic plot been lost in our own time as well? If the formal qualities of Attic tragedy were capable of being reinvented, can the same be true of the tragic plot?

A plot is what separates tragedy from history, or real life, even if real life is full of people trying to script lives for themselves or others. The horrific accident, random violence, or mere unhappiness are not "tragedies" in themselves, even though they make us profoundly sad. At the heart of tragedy is *pathos*, or suffering, which Aristotle defines in his usual offhanded sort of way as "a destructive or painful act, such as deaths on stage, paroxysms of pain, woundings and all that sort of thing" (37, 1452b10). The tragic plot can be taken to articulate a meaning for human suffering that does not emerge from the random mess of events. To put it another way, we seek meaning in tragedy, looking there for knowledge gained through suffering or simply the strange reassurance that what happened was necessary, that it had to be so. One must ask, of course, if to believe that something is necessary somehow makes it meaningful. Are we still left with the questions: why did it have to happen that way? Who said it should be so?

The necessity implied in tragedy evokes the inevitability inherent in the recounting of events that happened in real life, or what we call history. When telling the truth about the past, you cannot change it. Time cannot be reversed; therefore what happened appears in retrospect to be necessarily so. As Terry Eagleton describes it, "Tragedy is the present lived as though it were the past, tempering the excitement of a 'What comes next?' with the consoling certitudes of an ending we read back at each point into the evolving action" (102). But tragedy is different from history, insofar as the tragic poet always has the power to make things end differently, to allow for an ending that suits what we feel should happen, not what does happen.

The moralization of tragedy reveals the power of the idea of necessity, when what is seen as what *could* happen comes to have the force of what *has* happened. But what determines that necessity? What gives it such a terrifying strength? Aristotle calls that kind of necessity probability, but in Greek tragedy, the more powerful and darker word for it is *daimon*. *Daimon* is a kind of divinity manifested in a man or woman's life – and mostly for the worse. In tragedy, the ambiguity of the power of *daimon* can best be seen in the context of Heraclitus' dictum, "*ethos anthropoi daimon*," a phrase balancing the Greek word for character (*ethos*) with *daimon*, as the power to define the human being (*anthropos*): "For there to be tragedy it must be possible for the text simultaneously to imply two things: It is his character, in man, that one calls *daimon*, and conversely, what one calls character, in man, is in reality a *daimon*" (Vernant and Vidal-Naquet: 36–7). *Daimon* is both inside and outside of us, when it drives us either to happiness or disaster.

A broader term for necessity that impels human affairs is fate: the Greek words are *ananke* or *moira*. We usually think of fate as a force external to the tragic characters: however, as Northrop Frye puts it, "Fate, in a tragedy, normally becomes external to the hero only *after* the tragic process has been set going. The Greek *ananke* or *moira* is in its normal or pre-tragic form the internal balancing condition of life. It appears as external or antithetical necessity only after it has been violated as a condition of life" (210). That is, tragedy only exists in the tension between freedom and necessity, aligned with the tension between *ethos* and *daimon*. Paradoxically, the power of fate only becomes clear – and becomes tragic – in the moment of resistance to it. Freedom and necessity are mutually defined and constituted, and cannot exist without each other (see Eagleton: 115–19).

This chapter outlines some basic models and features of tragic plots in its evolution since the Greeks. Aristotle famously marked two aspects of Greek tragic plots as critical to the success of any tragedy: *peripeteia*, or reversal, and *anagnorisis*, or recognition. While Aristotle's definitions of these concepts are quite narrow, they provide a useful point of departure to name two kinds of tragic plot: the tragedy of the reversal of fortune, in which the protagonist experiences a catastrophic change in the direction of his or her life, and the tragedy of knowledge, in which the tragic character comes, often through a passage of suffering, to an insight into the human condition. Another important feature of the Greek tragic plot that Aristotle does not emphasize is the *agon*, or a conflict between characters. It is such conflict between two powerfully opposed wills or passions that often triggers the tragic catastrophe in what I would call the tragedy of desire. Tragic plots are also often driven by plotters, divine and human, who are present in the story, in this way exposing the mechanisms of necessity and the tension between character and fate. The chapter concludes with a consideration of Samuel Beckett's *Waiting for Godot* as a commentary on the tragic plot.

Reversal: The Tragedy of Fortune

Fundamentally, tragedy evokes a crisis in which everything changes, inexorably. Epics and novels also follow the turns of human experience, but in these genres the story unfolds over an extended period of time, whereas in tragedy, the change can be unbearably sudden and intense. Aristotle recognizes a change in fortune (*metabasis*) as the essence of a tragic plot; that is, in tragedy "a shift takes place either probably or necessarily from bad to good fortune or from good to bad" (31, 1451a10). The change is realized in the *peripeteia*, which Aristotle defines with almost comic abstraction: "'Peripety' [*peripeteia*] is a shift of what is being undertaken to the opposite in the way previously stated" (35, 1452a20). This definition would imply that it does not matter which way one's fortune changes, as long as it shifts somehow, but Aristotle does grudgingly recognize that the most "artistic" plot will "involve a change not from bad fortune to good fortune but the other way around, and from good fortune to bad, not thanks to wickedness but because of some mistake [*hamartia*] of great weight and consequence" (38, 1453a10–1453a15). In these few apparently offhand words is packed a great deal of controversy. No one questions the notion that it is better for tragedy to show a shift from good fortune to bad, but there is a great deal of dispute about the cause of the shift, which is said to be not wickedness but rather *hamartia*, or error.

Much of tragedy's evolution hinges on this question: who or what indeed is to blame for the tragic fall? We are impelled to ask "why," and tragedy so often frustrates us with its answer. In the following chapter on tragic heroes I will examine in more detail the concept of *hamartia* in relationship to tragic heroism, insofar as critics have transformed *hamartia* into not what the protagonist does but something inherent in his or her character (the so-called tragic flaw). Greek tragedy does reflect a highly complex construction of causality and guilt in ancient Athenian culture, and here I can touch on only the basics of the elaborate intertwining of collective and individual guilt and divine agency in tragic plots. One helpful way of outlining the issue is to compare two sets of tragedies that play out these issues: Aeschylus' *Oresteia* (seen as a trilogy) and Sophocles' *Oedipus the King* (seen as a single play, but with an eye to the other plays that Sophocles wrote about the suffering of the house of Laius).

The *Oresteia* knits a baroque chain of causality, both human and divine. Each play is distinct, but the three are linked by a set of horrific acts that trigger more disasters. Driving the events that we witness on the stage is a primal cause: the curse of Thyestes on the house of Atreus, as a revenge for Atreus' forcing him to eat his own children's flesh (which was retaliation for Thyestes' seduction of his own wife). In the next generation, Atreus' son, Agamemnon, goes to Troy, but at the cost of the sacrifice of his daughter, Iphigenia. In *Agamemnon*, the first play of the trilogy, the hero-general returns home to his wife Clytemnestra, who is seething with rage at her daughter's death. She murders her husband and his paramour Cassandra and declares herself and her lover Aegisthus (the son of Thyestes) rulers of Argos. In the second play, *The Libation Bearers*, Clytemnestra, in turn, is killed by her son Orestes as revenge for the death of his father. Orestes is then driven from Argos to Athens by the rage of the Furies, who punish matricides. It is only in the third play, *The Eumenides*, that a resolution is achieved. Athena convenes a jury of men to adjudicate the case, acquit Orestes, and placate the Furies. The shape of the plot of the first two plays is a spectacular descent, the fall of both the king in his triumphant glory on his return from war and of the queen who rules in the glory of her revenge. The protagonists appear overwhelmed by events over which they have no control, stemming from the power of the curse, while at the same time they are not absolved of personal responsibility for their actions. Only Athena's divine intervention, expressed in the civic mechanism of the court of the Areopagus, can break the cycle of revenge.

In contrast to the *Oresteia*, in *Oedipus the King*, the engine behind the chain of events is both invisible and morally incomprehensible. For Aristotle, *Oedipus the King* was a paradigmatic tragedy, especially for its exquisite simultaneity of the moment of reversal of fortune and the act of recognition: that is, Oedipus' fall coincides with his coming to know his own true identity. But for many post-classical readers this play serves as the paradigmatic "tragedy of fate," illustrating a man's inability to escape his own destiny, no matter how powerful or brilliant he might be. In the play it is critical that the oracle delivered at Delphi, prophesying that Oedipus will kill his father and marry his mother, must come true. Even as they praise their king, the chorus of the men of Thebes beg for it to be so, for the fulfillment of the oracles sustains their sense of order and meaning in the world:

> Never again will I go reverent to Delphi,
> The inviolate heart of Earth
> or Apollo's ancient oracle at Abae
> or Olympia of the fires –
> unless these prophecies all come true
> for all mankind to point to in wonder . . .
> They are dying, the old oracles sent to Laius,
> Now our masters strike them off the rolls.
> Nowhere Apollo's golden glory now –
> the gods, the gods go down. (210)

But as Bernard Knox has argued, a reading of the play as a testimony to the power of fate and helplessness of man often depends on confusing the myth with the plot of the play (1957: ch. 5). Whereas in the myth Oedipus might be perceived as the passive object of the gods' whims, driven from place to place until he meets his destiny in Thebes, what we see in the play is quite a different sort of action. Who is the plotter in this mostly intensely plot-driven play? Is the plot shaped by the gods or by the relentless, driving character of Oedipus himself?

One could say that there would not be a play without Oedipus, who directs the action, summons most of the characters to appear, and keeps the inquiry into the murder of Laius going when everyone else wants it to stop. The play foregrounds his agency at every moment, even after he has come to discover the truth of who he is. When Oedipus emerges from the palace after having blinded himself, he simultaneously insists on his status as the victim of the gods and the agent of his own destruction. When the chorus asks, "Dreadful, what you've done . . . how could you bear it, gouging out your eyes? / What superhuman power drove you on?" Oedipus answers, "Apollo, friends, Apollo – / he ordained my agonies – these, my pains on pains! / But the hand that struck my eyes was mine, / mine alone – no one else – I / I did it all myself!" (240–1). As Knox comments, "the autonomy of Oedipus' action allows Sophocles to present us not with a hero who is destroyed, but one who destroys himself" (*Oedipus at Thebes*: 51). The *Oresteia* binds together the protagonist's responsibility for his or her actions with the power of *daimon*, since Agamemnon and Clytemnestra are both possessed by the curse and act because of their own desires. *Oedipus the King*, in contrast, poses an insoluble conflict between what the hero must do, by the will of the gods, and what he desires, until he must take his destiny into his own hands and blind himself. While later critics of tragedy will strive somehow to find the cause of Oedipus' fall in himself, in his pride or anger, in the end there is no good answer as to why the gods brought this destiny upon Oedipus.

The obsession with human catastrophes has never left Western culture. It survived through the Roman re-creation of Greek tragedy, and even with the hiatus of the production of tragedy from the fall of the Roman Empire to the Italian Renaissance, the idea of the tragic as a reversal of fortune doggedly persisted. In medieval literary theory the notion of tragedy was reborn in the image of the inexorable turn of Fortune's wheel, which eventually grinds all those who sit at the top of the world into dust. In the prologue to the Monk's Tale in *The Canterbury Tales*, Chaucer offers a simple definition of tragedy: "Tragedie is to seyn a certeyn storie, / As olde bookes maken us memoire, / Of hym that stood in greet prosperitee, / And is yfallen out of heigh degree, / Into myserie, and endeth wrecchedly" (241). As in Aristotle's *Poetics*, Chaucer's definition ties tragedy to a change in a person's life from prosperity to misery – but not for everyone. For Chaucer, tragedy only happens to those of "high degree," or of wealth and high social rank. In his translation of Boethius, Chaucer names the agent of the change, in insisting, "What other thynge bywaylen the cryinges of tragedyes but oonly the dedes of Fortune, that with an unwar strook overturneth the realmes of greet nobleye?" (409). That is, Fortune made it happen. At the end of the Monk's Tale Chaucer seems to suggest that Fortune's work is more than random, for it attacks mostly the "proude," for "that Fortune alwey wole assaille / With unwar strook the regnes that been proude; / For whan men trusteth hire, thanne wol she faille, / And covere hire brighte face with a clowde" (252). Medieval tragic theory thus may suggest the evenhandedness of Fortune's machinery, which assails all; yet it also repositions the tragic plot in a charged context, where tragedy displays the punishment of the proud, and especially kings and princes.

The classical tragic reversal also maps nicely onto the Christian image of our fall from grace: the sin of Adam and Eve and the loss of Paradise. This story was reproduced repeatedly in the European morality plays of the fourteenth and fifteenth centuries. These allegorical plays are characterized by a plot of temptation, fall, and redemption, often centered on the fate of a single protagonist, who may be a figure of mankind, a king, or a youth whose soul is endangered. Forces of good and evil battle for the soul of that central figure, who stands for all of us. He is usually brought from a state of prosperity to despair by a figure called "Vice" or by his surrogates of sin. The protagonist may be saved in the end, but only by the forces of mercy or grace. In establishing this scheme for an ethical drama of reversal, the morality play set a pattern for later vernacular drama that both overlapped and conflicted with that plot of reversal of fortune. While in the case of classical tragedy and the tragedy of fortune, the cause of the turn of events is mystified, in the morality play it is obsessively displayed in both the agents of temptation and the choice of the protagonist to choose to sin. W. H. Auden defined Greek tragedy as the tragedy of necessity and Christian tragedy as the tragedy of possibility, since the emphasis on the *choice* to sin suggests it could be otherwise (1). Christianity always holds out the possibility of redemption and raises questions of how there can be a true tragedy in a world governed by providence rather than fate.

Christopher Marlowe's *The Tragical History of Doctor Faustus* is a play modeled on the tradition of the morality play, full of the morality machinery, including a baleful Lucifer, Mephistopheles, and good and bad angels. Yet its plot of reversal is curiously misaligned with the morality pattern of either demonstrating the turn of Fortune's wheel, or the temptation, fall, and redemption of "mankind." Marlowe's play is based on a lurid contemporary source, the "Faustbook," a popular account of the magical feats and misdeeds of Johannes Faustus, a German necromancer. In his dramatic re-creation of the tale of Faustus, Marlowe combines several models of the tragic experience: the fall of Icarus, the rebellion of the angels, and the temptation of Everyman. As the prologue puts it, in the play we see how Faustus, "excelling all whose sweet delight disputes / In heavenly matters of theology; / Till swoll'n with cunning, of a self-conceit / His waxen wings did mount above his reach, / And melting heavens conspired his overthrow" (6–7, Prologue.18–22). At the beginning Faustus deliberately chooses to sell his soul to Lucifer in exchange for magical powers. The play proceeds to unfold the implications of that choice, as Faustus performs marvelous and then trivial spells, while he is tormented by his conscience, staged in the form of good and bad angels who vie for his attention. In the end, it is unclear if indeed Faustus could have been saved by mercy or grace, or if he was damned from the first and thus the play is just a relentless demonstration of that fact. The play brilliantly challenges the morality pattern of tragic temptation and fall, even as it mimics it, for even though agency of the devil is so conspicuously displayed on stage, we never really know what drives Faustus to his damnation (see Dollimore).

The conflated medieval and classical inheritance of Renaissance tragedy blends tragic reversal with a profound doubt about its causes. Where Philip Sidney grapples with both the vernacular tradition and emergent neoclassicism in *The Defence of Poesy*, he defends tragedy as a politically didactic genre: how could one object, he asks, to

> high and excellent Tragedy, that openeth the greatest wounds, and showeth forth the ulcers that are covered with tissue; that maketh kings fear to be tyrants, and tyrants to manifest their tyrannical humours; that, with stirring the affects of admiration of commiseration, teacheth the uncertainty of this world, and upon how weak foundations gilden roofes are builded. (98)

In Sidney's thinking, the world we live in may be uncertain, but what is certain is that the proud build on weak foundations and tyrants will fall. Political tragedies flourished in the English Renaissance, building on the vernacular model of the genre of the "mirror for magistrates" meant to demonstrate the consequences of political venality or pride.

In the two versions of *King Lear* that survive, one labels the play *The Tragedy of King Lear* and another *The History of King Lear*. This confusion not only suggests the instability of generic labels in Shakespeare's time (if it's a history, do we know how it might end?), but it also suggests a fundamental crux at the play's core: why does Cordelia die? Shakespeare boldly alters the outlines of the Lear–Cordelia story from all the known versions in his time. In those versions Cordelia defeats her wicked sisters, and she and the King of France restore her father to the throne, where he reigns again until he dies of old age. She rules after him until she is overthrown by her nephews and commits suicide. In Shakespeare's play, however, both Lear and Cordelia die at the play's end; in violation of history's message, the conclusion is profoundly tragic.

The brutality and apparent senselessness of this ending are put into relief by the Edmund–Edgar–Gloucester subplot, which follows the more traditional turn of the "wheel of fortune" plot while it conveys the sense that the wheel is powered by a kind of moral authority or necessity. When Edgar exacts his revenge against his evil half-brother Edmund, Edmund himself recognizes that now "the wheel is come full circle" (5.3.175). Edgar announces to his brother regarding his father's punishment: "The gods are just, and of our pleasant vices / Make instruments to plague us: / The dark and vicious place where thee he got / Cost him his eyes" (5.3.171–3). The wheel has turned – but with a sense of purpose.

In the Lear plot, however, the reversal is more complex. First, unlike historical tragedies such as *Richard II* or *Richard III* that culminate in a king's overthrow, *Lear* begins, quite perversely, with a king overthrowing himself, that is, abdicating his throne to his three daughters, dividing the kingdom, and rejecting and banishing his most beloved child and his advisor Kent. All that then happens could be seen as ensuing from Lear's *hamartia*; yet the play obsessively asks *why* Lear should be abandoned and driven to madness. All the characters themselves ask why, and they supply many different answers. The wicked daughters, Goneril and Regan, have all too good an answer for this question: Lear has surrendered his power, and having done so, when he misbehaves, he should be punished. Lear himself cannot understand what has happened, because he believes so strongly in his own authority and invulnerability. Only after the night on the heath can he glimpse both his own mortality and culpability. Yet when Lear confesses his sin and asks Cordelia's forgiveness, appearing to close the circle of cause and effect, Cordelia complicates that closure by refusing his acceptance of blame: "No cause, no cause," she murmurs (4.7.74). Thus, an economy of crime and punishment is collapsed in a proleptically Christian moment of love and sacrifice. If the audience would then hope that this forgiveness foretells a comic redemption, we are most cruelly disappointed. The final image of Lear howling, with his daughter's dead body in his arms, is shattering. The Earl of Kent asks, "Is this the promis'd end?" (5.3.264). What had all the plot lines led us to believe that we were going to see? A happy ending? Or even a just ending?

Cordelia's death proved to be a test case for later audiences' responses to the tragedy of the reversal of fortune. Samuel Johnson confesses that "I was many years ago so shocked by Cordelia's death, that I know not whether I ever endured to read again the last scenes of the play till I undertook to revise them as an editor" (240). And indeed by the end of the seventeenth century Nahum Tate delivered to the world a new version of *King Lear* that ruled the stage for the next century and a half. In this version not only are the evil characters punished, but the good are also rewarded: Cordelia survives and is married off (with an admirable sense of poetic justice) to Edgar. By the end of the seventeenth century, the pressure for a tragedy to have a morally justified ending had become irresistible. For the neoclassical tragedians of seventeenth-century France, too, moral justice was essential, as the highest expression of decorum. In his preface to *Phèdre*, Jean Racine protests that he has never written a play that so celebrates virtue, where "the smallest faults are here severely punished; the mere idea of a crime is looked upon with as much horror as the crime itself" (23) (even though the play itself seems to transcend that kind of moral scruple).

At the end of the seventeenth century, English critical taste dictated a tragic economy of reward for virtue and punishment of vice, and eventually, this older kind of tragedy lost its audience, to be replaced by melodrama. One of the most influential treatises of the latter part of the seventeenth century was Thomas Rymer's "The Tragedies of the Last Age Consider'd" (1678), which observed the "necessary relation and chain, whereby the causes and the effects, the vertues and rewards, the vices and their punishments are proportion'd and link'd together; how deep and dark soever are laid the springs, and however intricate and involv'd are their operations" (75). Rymer strictly judged that the tragedies of the previous age – those of Shakespeare, for example – did not generally live up to this standard. Indeed they did not, a fact for which we are now quite grateful. The pressure for both bourgeois decorum and morality proved to be a straitjacket for tragedy, and few tragedies from this period survive today in the canon. George Lillo's play *The London Merchant* (1731) broke from the neoclassical model in featuring a tragedy of a middle-class man, but the story itself is purely homiletic. In this play a woman leads the young merchant George Barnwell astray to rob his employer and murder his uncle: in the end, crime does not pay, and he and the woman who seduced him are tried and executed. In the nineteenth-century theater audiences reveled in melodrama, plays enhanced by spectacle and music that put the virtuous characters in danger in the hands of criminals only to be miraculously saved at the last minute from what appears to be certain death.

The tragedy of the reversal of fortune might be said to live on today in at least two film genres: the disaster film and the biographical film (or "biopic"). The disaster film plays out the reversal of fortune on a grand scale, usually implying that the disaster – the shipwreck, the earthquake, the towering inferno – is at once both warranted and inexplicable. These modern disaster films characteristically follow stories of individuals affected by the calamity, but behind all of them looms the hubris of modern ambition: the arrogance that leads men to build the great ship or tall building that triggers the catastrophe. The immensely popular film *Titanic* is the most notable recent example of such a film. The ship itself and its makers are represented as culpable for the disaster that ensues, for the scale of the ship and their hubris in pushing forward even in the face of danger. Yet the film encompasses a myriad of interwoven stories of characters caught up and redefined in the crucible of the disaster. Good and evil characters are damned and a few are saved, but each one of them is defined by how they respond to the wreck. The frame of the film, which is the quest for a fabulous diamond which has gone missing, ends with a kind of ironic morality: if the quest is driven by greed, it ends with the heroine Rose returning the lost jewel to the ocean.

In contrast to the disaster film, the "biopic" focuses on the fall of an individual by titanic proportions, whether celebrity or criminal. As with the disaster film, the outcome of such films is characteristically over-determined: we *know* how they must end. Orson Welles's *Citizen Kane*, for example, is a uniquely modern version of the tragedy of the reversal of fortune. It begins, quite spectacularly and defiantly, with the hero's death and his last word, "Rosebud." Not only does the movie begin with the death of Kane, but it is followed quickly by the "March of Time" newsreel in which you see Kane's life unfold. What story is then left to be told? What proceeds is Kane's biography portrayed from multiple, overlapping perspectives, showing the different

Kanes of Mr. Thatcher (who demonstrates the relationship between Kane's life and money), Bernstein (who says it wasn't money Kane wanted), Leland (who relates Kane's selfishness), Susan Alexander (who insists "Everything was his idea"), and finally Raymond, Kane's butler, who pronounces, "He got everything he wanted and lost it." As in Greek tragedy, *Citizen Kane* retells a story that has already been told, so the tension lies not in discovering the ending, but in seeing how the ending will be achieved and in grasping the key to the meaning of Kane's life. The many explanations and perspectives are reinforced by the brilliant cinematography, which constantly offers multiple perspectives through windows, doorways, and mirrors. *Citizen Kane* foregrounds the interpretation of the reversal of fortune, obsessively displaying the human impulse to try to understand *why* such things happen.

Plotters: The Tragedy of Revenge

Often the tragic outcome seems inevitable, tied to the way that the story has always been told. In the words of the chorus in Anouilh's *Antigone*, the tragic plot seems like an engine that pulls the disaster to its conclusion: "The machine is in perfect order; it has been oiled ever since time began, and it runs without friction. . . . Tragedy is restful; and the reason is that hope, that foul, deceitful thing, has no part in it. There isn't any hope. You're trapped" (23–4). But many tragic plots also simultaneously lay bare the mechanisms in order to feature the actions of the plotter, who is both the agent and the object of tragedy.

In Greek tragedy, the gods themselves may be revealed as the plotters. In Euripides' *Hippolytus*, Aphrodite introduces the play as the fulfillment of her plan for revenge against Hippolytus for denying her powers. More significantly, Euripides' *The Bacchae* cruelly frames the tragic plot as both a revenge strategy and a means to prove the power of the gods. *The Bacchae* stages the breakdown of the city, representing Thebes as threatened from without but really from within (see Segal). It is fueled by a power struggle that exposes the means by which power is created and legitimized, especially through everything that Dionysus represents. The motivating force of the play is Dionysus' plan, which he announces in the prologue: he states that he has returned to Thebes to exact his revenge against those who denied his divinity and thus to prove he is a god. But how do you indeed *know* he is not an impostor, as Pentheus claims? The means Dionysus uses to establish his divinity are multiple: the ecstatic acclamation of the chorus celebrating the power of Dionysus, the "miracles" he is said to perform, and the sacrifice of Pentheus and humiliation of Agave. But at each moment, all that evidence is continually questioned: the miracles are reported rather than witnessed, and even when his power has been demonstrated, Cadmus and Agave question whether such is the kind of power that is appropriate to a god. The unsettling effect of the play is that we see what Sophocles disguises in his absent gods: the need for divine power to be ratified in the violent conclusion.

When the plotter is thus entangled in his own plot, causality becomes questionable, both morally and metaphysically. While *The Bacchae* exposes the irrationality that motivates the plot, Shakespeare's *Othello* explores the mystery of how a man can be driven to murder the woman he loves. Othello's elopement with Desdemona is the trigger for the plot, but the catastrophe is engineered by Iago, who manipulates appearances to make Othello believe that Desdemona is sleeping with Cassio, Othello's lieutenant. In a moment of cold madness, Othello strangles Desdemona and then kills himself. It is clear that the tragedy would never have happened without the agency of Iago as the tragic plotter. Time and again it appears as if the disaster could be averted, and Othello's faith in Desdemona sustained, but Iago applies another turn of the screw, and the machine grinds on.

In *The Bacchae* we know *why* Dionysus plots against Pentheus, but in Othello, Iago's reasons are obscure. Why does Iago so relentlessly pursue the destruction of Othello? Samuel Taylor Coleridge was the first critic to point to Iago's acts as the "motive-hunting of a motiveless malignity" (113). Iago himself seems uncertain as to why he is doing this, since in his soliloquies he gives several inconsistent reasons, including Othello's having preferred Cassio as his lieutenant, his jealousy from believing that Othello has slept with his own wife (though he undercuts this), and his own lust for Desdemona. Iago's motivation is both over-determined and self-contradictory to the extent that he becomes less a psychologically coherent character than the figure of malignity or evil itself. Dazed after realizing the truth of what Iago has done, Othello looks at Iago's feet to see if they are cloven like the devil's hooves. In the early morality plays, a demonic figure called Vice orchestrates the appearance of the various sins and interacts with the audience, as Iago does, drawing them into his perspective as a plotter. In this sense, Iago becomes Vice transfigured into a named character. The will of the gods in Greek tragedy, as represented in their oracles, may be at best amoral. In *Othello*, divine will becomes malignity or evil, which drags civilization down to barbarism.

Recognizing the power of revenge in *The Bacchae* and *Othello* leads back to tragedy's beginning, to the *Oresteia*, where acts of violence span more intolerable cruelty, seemingly out of control, not in the hands of any single character, low or high. The chain of horrors that is the *Oresteia* begins long before the action of the play, with the transgressions of Thyestes and Atreus, which becomes a miasma that infects all of the house of Atreus. It is ended with the establishment of the court of the Areopagus and the appeasement of the hideous Furies, who embody the spirit of revenge for familial crimes, but this is clearly an imposition of the will of Athena. As Francis Bacon wrote:

> Revenge is a kind of wild justice; which the more man's nature runs to, the more ought law to weed it out. For as for the first wrong, it doth but offend the law; but the revenge of that wrong putteth the law out of office. Certainly, in taking revenge, a man is but even with his enemy; but in passing it over, he is superior; for it is a prince's part to pardon. (347)

Bacon's words point to the anxiety about moral and political authority at the heart of any tragic plot shaped by revenge. The revenger, who can be seen as a figure of the playwright, attempts to wrest control of the action from the corrupt authorities, usually with the result that the revenger becomes contaminated by the violence that he or she abhors.

The flourishing of revenge tragedy in early modern England is a symptom of a society in transition, where traditional forms of authority and the nature of law were being questioned (see Maus). The time fit well with the rediscovery of Senecan tragedy, dominated by tyrants and haunted by ghosts calling for revenge, peaking with Thomas Newton's 1581 edition of the *Tenne Tragedies* of Seneca, translated into English by several different authors (the translations themselves date from 1559–66). The pattern for English revenge tragedy was set by Thomas Kyd's *The Spanish Tragedy* (ca. 1587). The plot of the play is introduced by the all too Senecan ghost of Don Andrea and a character called Revenge who seeks retribution for Andrea's murder by Don Balthazar. As Revenge announces, "Here sit we down to see the mystery, / And serve for Chorus in this tragedy" (9, 1.1.91–2). But no one directly avenges Andrea's death; rather, the play follows the schemes of Hieronomo, a justice in the court of Castile, who wants justice for the murder of his son Horatio, also killed by Balthazar and Lorenzo, the prince of Castile. Unlike his successor, Hamlet, who was only mad "north by northwest," Hieronimo goes truly mad in his frustration with his inability to achieve that justice. In the end, the only way he can accomplish his revenge is by staging a play in which the mimed violence turns real. At the climax, with the onstage spectators still witless, Hieronimo displays the body of his son and tells the story, but then he bites out his own tongue and stabs himself. In the final scene the ghost of Andrea tries to tidy up the significance of all these grisly deaths, sorting out the just from the unjust, but finally they are all merely "spectacles to please my soul" (122, 4.5.12). The final effect of the revenge tragedy is to empty out the meaning of justice and to institute the rule of violence and death. Language fails, the distinction between play and reality disappears, and all collapses into the pleasures of "sweet violence."

The Spanish Tragedy had a significant after-effect in its own time, most famously in Shakespeare's *Hamlet* – a play that adapted the revenge-play conventions and turned them inside out. *Hamlet* is a revenge tragedy that questions every aspect and convention of the revenge-tragedy plot while it reproduces them. The play interrogates why revenge motivates a plot, not by directly questioning the value of revenge, but simply by deferring it. Hamlet is as puzzled as we are by his delays, especially when he sees his own case refracted in those of Laertes and Fortinbras. The Ghost who demands that Hamlet "Remember me" becomes both a terrifying psychological presence and a provoker of metaphysical questions: what is he, why should we believe him, and what, then, should Hamlet do that is right? At the crux of the play is the very nature of tragic action and its causality – the "divinity that shapes our ends, / Rough-hew them how we will" (5.2.10–11). All the revenge plays of the English Renaissance – including *The Revenger's Tragedy, Antonio's Revenge, Titus Andronicus, The Jew of Malta*, and *The Revenge of Bussy D'Ambois* – open up this void of understanding of what it means to act in a corrupt society where even religion has lost its certitude (see Neill).

Revenge's power to shape a tragic plot has never really waned, whether it is because people have never stopped lusting for vengeance or because we continue to be fascinated by their mechanisms of plotting. Romantic tragedy is rife with revenge plots. The heroes of Friedrich Schiller and Victor Hugo tend to be tormented rebels whose identities are shaped by their desire for revenge against a king or rival who has robbed them of their birthright. Thus, the revenge plot allows for the exploration of political or social themes. Twentieth-century playwrights were attracted to the theme of the *Oresteia*, and especially to the idea of a paralyzing miasma of guilt from violence. In *Mourning Becomes Electra*, Eugene O'Neill translated the *Oresteia* into the world of nineteenth-century America, transforming the primal curse on the house of Atreus into psychic compulsion.

A more recent manifestation of the longevity of the tragic revenge plot is the success of Francis Ford Coppola's *Godfather* trilogy, which follows a struggle for power and a cycle of violence that originates in the assassination of the father of young Vito Corleone. The *Godfather* films are gangster films, but their world is shaped by a culture invested in family honor and loyalty (see Man). While the plot may start with Vito Corleone, the trilogy belongs to Michael Corleone, his son. Michael begins like the classic revenger, who believes that he cannot be stained by the crimes of his predecessors (as he says to his wife Kay, "That's my family, Kay. It's not me"). However, inescapably, he becomes the most calculating plotter, responsible for deaths both inside and outside the family. The next two films of the trilogy follow the collapse of his family authority, as well as of his domination of the world of the mob. The revenge plot may thus question the "official" world of civic justice, which is powerless to right social wrongs, but it also destabilizes the mythology of an alternative structure of power – here the power of the "family" and the "mob."

Recognition: The Tragedy of Knowledge

The revenge tragedy may initiate an exploration of the mystery of human desire, but the revenger rarely understands himself or his world, until it is too late. But such plays remind us that at the heart of tragedy we find a crisis of knowledge. Aristotle especially admired plays where the change of fortune (*perepeteia*) coincides with recognition (*anagnorisis*), as it does in *Oedipus the King*. The *Poetics* defines recognition narrowly, as "a shift from ignorance to awareness, pointing in the direction either of close blood ties or of hostility, of people who have been in a clearly marked state of happiness or unhappiness" (36, 1452a30). The best recognition emerges naturally from the plot, as, for example, the recognition of Orestes in *The Libation Bearers*, which is based on reasoning, or the recognition accomplished by a letter in *Iphigenia in Tauris*.

This plot device is a symptom of the importance in tragedy of the discovery of knowledge. According to Terence Cave, post-Aristotelian tragic criticism shifted the focus from recognition's role as part of a tragic situation to the protagonist's experience. In this context, recognition signaled inner awareness or inner knowledge and not just coming to know your relations (153). Recognition thus embraces knowing the truth of your relationships, knowing who you really are, and, ultimately, knowing the truth of human existence.

The *Oresteia* implies that tragic knowledge is inseparable from the experience of reversal. We have seen the ways in which the *Oresteia* traces out a series of catastrophes, the fall of Agamemnon, the murder of Clytemnestra, and the contamination of Orestes, culminating in the untying of the knot of blood guilt in the final play. But the *Oresteia* is also punctuated by important acts of recognition, literal and figurative. At the beginning of *Agamemnon*, the chorus of old Argive men sings of the ravages of the Trojan War and of a generational war among the gods, ending in Zeus' victory. Through this pain "Zeus has led us on to know, / the Helmsman lays it down as law / that we must suffer, suffer into truth [*ton phronein brotous odosanta, ton pathei mathos*]" (109). Robert Fagles comments on this passage: "Perhaps no paradox inspired Aeschylus more than the bond that might exist between *pathos* and *mathos*, suffering and its significance. That bond is life itself" (16). To make a bookend to the old men's evocation of *pathos/mathos*, Fagles translates a later set of lines for Orestes to fulfill that mandate: his Orestes declares in the face of the Furies who threaten to drag him down into agony, "I have suffered into truth" (243). However, the Greek is a little different: "*ego didaktheis en kakois epistamai.*" Literally translated this means: "I understand, having been educated, through evils (*kakois*)." Orestes follows with an account of his having learned the ritual of purging, when to speak, and when to be silent. It is not clear that Orestes' act of learning, or coming to understand, is the same as "coming to the truth." What the text tells us is that through the experience of *pathos* and *kakos*, suffering and evil, we learn, but it does not tell us *what* we learn. We still must ask: what are the implications of connecting knowledge with tragic suffering?

In *The Libation Bearers* a sequence of Aristotelian recognition scenes connect knowledge with both kinship and death. Electra must recognize Orestes, who has returned from exile to murder his mother as revenge for his father's death, by matching their locks of hair. Clytemnestra first fails to recognize her son when he returns in disguise. Clytemnestra recognizes him first through an act of violence: his murder of her lover Aegisthus. Recognition, in this case, involves the paradox of blood ties in this family. What binds the family in love also yokes them together in hatred. In the end, the truth is mysterious and cruel. Robert Fagles sees the *Oresteia* ultimately as optimistic, as a "rite of passage from savagery to civilization" (Aeschylus 1985: 19), citing Thomas Hardy that " 'if way to the Better there be, it exacts a full look at the Worst' " (16). One is left wondering, however, if in this mystification of the promise of knowledge lurks the justification or even celebration of suffering.

The truth suffered by the characters of Greek tragedy is not the kind of truth that can guide you in life. It is more like the truth that Oedipus discovers in *his* horrific moment of recognition, when he comes to see that his wife is his mother, and that he is the one who murdered the king, his father. Thus, he discovers the "truth" that oracles must be fulfilled. This is a truth that is a horror; it has nothing to do with moral rectitude, justice, or the good. It is simply a truth that represents the will of the gods and the inescapable fact of what has already happened. *Oedipus the King* demonstrates both the power and agony inherent in the search for knowledge. In his moral quest to discover the identity of Laius, Oedipus finds that there are necessary consequences of that discovery – murder and incest. What kind of truth is it, indeed, that is uncovered as a result of this tragedy?

In *The Birth of Tragedy* Friedrich Nietzsche further mystifies the notion of the tragic truth. For him, tragedy is the crucible of art that heals the terrible wound of a vision into the depths of existence. His "Dionysiac man," the life force of tragedy, recognizes that truth:

> In this sense Dionysiac man is similar to Hamlet: both have gazed into the true essence of things, they have *acquired knowledge* and they find

action repulsive, for their actions can do nothing to change the eternal essence of things. . . . Once truth has been seen, the consciousness of it prompts man to see only what is terrible or absurd in existence wherever he looks. (40)

Tragedy emerges from the encounter of that vision with the "Apollonian" shaping power of art, with at its heart a truth so powerful it can blind or burn.

But let us look at *Hamlet*, on its own terms. One could compare Hamlet to both the *Oresteia* and *Oedipus the King*, as it is a tragedy of knowledge as well as a revenge tragedy. Like both works, *Hamlet* begins with the death of a king. In *Oedipus* and *Hamlet*, the death takes place before the play begins, whereas in *Agamemnon* it is enacted. Agamemnon's death is no mystery, but the deaths of Laius and Old Hamlet are. In *Oedipus* and *Hamlet* we might think at first, as the heroes do, that the present crisis could be solved if you could find the murderer and then avenge the death of the king. However, that is exactly not the case. The chorus first thinks that discovering who murdered Laius will cure Thebes of the plague that ravages it, but that can be done only by finding the plague in the heart of the King of Thebes. While Hamlet knows that his world is out of joint, or rotten, he does not even know at first that there was a murder. He knows only that his father is dead and his mother has married his uncle. The twist in the play comes, early on, when the ghost tells him who killed his father. Thus, the truth that is the climax for Oedipus is the beginning of a frustrated plot of revenge for Hamlet. It is implied that there is a far deeper truth that he must discover.

In the play, Hamlet relentlessly questions himself and others, and he is questioned, in turn. Everyone asks: what is he thinking? What does he want? So Hamlet accuses Rosencrantz and Guildenstern: "You would play upon me; you would seem to know my stops; you would pluck out the heart of my mystery" (3.2.372–4). The lesson for Hamlet and for all those who question him is that they cannot know: anyone who wants to play the detective will end up dead. As for Hamlet, he learns to stop asking questions. When Hamlet has misgivings about the upcoming duel with Laertes, Horatio begs him to question this feeling and avoid the fight. But Hamlet protests: "Not a whit, we defy augury. There is special providence in the fall of a sparrow. If it be [now], 'tis not to come; if it be not to come, it will be now; if it be not now, yet it [will] come – the readiness is all" (5.2.219–22). In the First Folio version of the text, Hamlet continues with a question: "Since no man ha's ought of what he leaues. What is't to leaue betimes?" But the equivalent lines from the Second Quarto answer Hamlet's question of "to or not to be": "Since no man of ought he leaues, knowes what ist to leaue betimes, let be" (See *The Three-Text Hamlet*: 244–7). The Second Quarto version of the line effectively ties together Hamlet's sacrifice the control of knowledge and his own fate. Read in the context of the biblical reference to God's will in the fall of the sparrow (Matthew 10:29), Hamlet's defiance of augury seems not like defiance at all, but an act of acknowledgment. Hamlet sees the disregard of presentiment for what it amounts to: the willingness to suffer the future. He gains the knowledge of the unintelligibility of our destiny, a dark mystery that the living cannot know.

As men of extraordinary intelligence who confront the irrationality of destiny, Hamlet and Oedipus foreshadow the character of the detective-hero driven to discover a truth that, in the end, he cannot fully comprehend. In his short essay "The Simple Art of Murder," Raymond Chandler describes the detective as a man of integrity surviving in a corrupt world:

> Down these mean streets a man must go who is not himself mean, who is neither tarnished nor afraid. The detective in this kind of story must be such a man, . . . The story is his adventure in search of a hidden truth, and it would be no adventure if it did not happen to a man fit for adventure. He has a range of awareness that startles you, but it belongs to him by right, because it belongs to the world he lives in. (991–2)

But what is the "hidden truth" the hero finds, through the chaos of death, both purposeful and random? For Sam Spade, in Dashiel Hammett's *The Maltese Falcon*, it is a statue made of lead, a fraud.

The antitype of Chandler's brave hero is Mike Hammer, in the corrosive film noir, *Kiss Me Deadly*, where the consequences of the search for truth are catastrophic. Hammer is sent on his quest by the last words of the mysterious hitchhiker Christina, the same words that the ghost delivers to Hamlet: "Remember me." These words impel Hammer, almost unwittingly, to seek to know what they mean. The answer is the object that Hammer's girlfriend Velda calls "the great whatsit," some kind of thermonuclear bomb. But it is not a thing so much as the discovery of knowledge itself that motivates Hammer's quest, and in the end, it is not the bomb, but this search for knowledge that destroys everyone. When Hammer realizes that his quest has placed the bomb, as well as his girlfriend Velda, in the wrong hands, he stammers guiltily, "I didn't know." His friend, policeman Lt. Pat Murphy, replies, "You didn't know. You think you'd have done any different if you had known?" The spectacular climax, steeped in classical allusions to Medusa's head and Pandora's box, comes when the villainess Gabrielle opens the box that contains the bomb, unleashing the power of nuclear fission in the world and (in the original version) destroying villains and heroes alike.

A more contemporary version of the film noir detective-hero is Jake Gittes, in Roman Polanski's *Chinatown*. In this film, Chinatown represents "the unknowable" (Naremore: 206). Gittes is told to do "as little as possible" in Chinatown. The District Attorney is said to have warned him, "You may think you know what's going on, but you don't." Following the evasive and enticing Evelyn Mulwray, Gittes never seems to find what he thinks he is going to find. What he does find is the corruption both at the heart of Los Angeles – the manipulation of water – and at the heart of the Mulwray family, the secret of the incest between Evelyn Mulwray and her father Noah Cross (in an eerie echo of Oedipus). Gittes persistently misunderstands the situation as he seeks the truth, and his efforts to protect Evelyn and her daughter lead to Evelyn's death. The first version of the script by Robert Towne had an ending in which Cross was killed and Evelyn's daughter was saved, but in Polanski's final version the film ends with Evelyn dead and Noah Cross embracing her daughter, threatening the repetition of incest. Gittes is handcuffed to the man who has, in Oedipal fashion, shot Evelyn in the eye. In this modern version of the tragedy of knowledge, the discovery of the truth – of Noah Cross's political and sexual crimes – is not redemptive. Instead Gittes's discovery draws him, Evelyn, and her daughter into Cross's net of lies and manipulation. It is a profoundly pessimistic vision.

The Agon: The Tragedy of Desire

One element of the Greek tragic plot that Aristotle neglects is the *agon*: an episode of intense dialogue or confrontation between two characters that defines a tragic conflict of values, wills, or desires. He may not have focused on it because (unlike recognition) the *agon*, in its narrowest definition, lacks an explicit connection to the reversal of fortune. Yet almost all Greek tragedies include such a scene of confrontation, and such episodes often crystallize the conflict that fuels the catastrophe (Lloyd: 2). Think, for example, of the vicious and profoundly serious debate between Antigone and Creon at the heart of *Antigone*. When the sentry presents his prize, Antigone, as the criminal who buried Polynices, Creon turns violently on her, demanding that she confess. She does so in a speech that declares her allegiance to the "great, unshakable traditions" that require the burial of blood kind. Creon retaliates, interestingly enough, not by defending his own principles of loyalty to the state, but by attacking Antigone as a stubborn and insolent girl who must be broken. That speech is followed by an intense round of *stichomythia*, attack and counter-attack, between the two, broken up only by the entrance of Antigone's sister Ismene, who becomes a magnet for their mutual anger. At the end of this scene, all that is settled is that Antigone must die.

In his extensive analysis of the *agon* in Euripides' plays, Michael Lloyd observes how the tragic *agon* reflects the agonistic nature of Greek intellectual and political life, where political and legal discourse were structured around constant debate. Jean-Pierre Vernant and Pierre Vidal-Naquet point to the omnipresence of legal terminology and argumentation in Greek tragedy that ties the genre to that culture of debate. All of this argument is directed toward coming to understand our place in "a world that is at once social, natural, divine, and ambiguous, rent by contradictions, in which no rule appears definitively established, one god fights against another, one law against another and in which, even in the course of the play's action, justice itself shifts, twists, and is transformed into its contrary" (32).

Neoclassical tragic theory followed Aristotle in ignoring the *agon*, but later critics refocused tragedy on conflict, with the result that *Antigone* took precedence over *Oedipus the King* as a model. Above all, the philosopher Georg Wilheim Friedrich Hegel was responsible for naming the conflict of values as the essence of tragedy. In his *Lectures on Fine Art (Vorlesungen über die Ästhetik)*, Hegel formulates ethical conflict as the basis of the tragic experience, whether on the level of the individual, acting in self-defense, or on a broader stage, as he saw it played out in *Antigone:*

The chief conflict treated most beautifully by Sophocles, with Aeschylus as his predecessor, is that between the state, i.e. ethical life in its *spiritual* universality, and the family, i.e. *natural* ethical life. These are the clearest powers that are presented in tragedy, because the full reality of ethical existence consists in harmony between these two spheres. (1213)

To put it another way, Hegel saw as the catalyst for the crisis of Greek tragedy, not fate or the recovery or recognition of a terrible knowledge, but simply the irreconcilable conflict of two equal and opposed sets of values. As Silk and Stern comment on the Hegelian conflict: "There is no blindness or ignorance. There is no crime. The absolute tragic conflict is the conflict of two all but fully informed consciousnesses, two agents who all but fully understand themselves and each other, and who oppose each other by the assertion and counter-assertion of valid but conflicting laws" (317–18).

The easiest way to demonstrate this tension in *Antigone* is to ask: "So, who is the hero of this play?" You don't have to ask this question about *Oedipus the King* or *King Lear*, but the question of "who is the hero" of *Antigone* drives the respondent to declare, "whose side are you on?" Antigone appears from the start as the rebel, thus engaging the sympathies of those who instinctively connect rebellion against established authority with the side of justice. But Antigone does not defend new ideas against the entrenched ways of the old, but rather an ancient right to bury one's kin. So she defies Creon: "Nor did I think your edict had such force / that you, a mere mortal, could override the gods, / the great unwritten, unshakable traditions" (82). Creon, however, argues on behalf of the state's interest and *its* right to punish traitors: "These are my principles. Never at my hands / will the traitor be honored above the patriot. / But whoever proves his loyalty to the state: / I'll prize that man in death as well as life" (68). The play refuses to declare a clear winner. Even though Antigone does die and in that sense Creon is victorious, Creon too is defeated by the suicides of his wife and son, and in the end, he is a shell, "no one. Nothing" (126).

The conflict in *Antigone* itself is more than about just family and state; fundamentally it erupts in the tension between desire and the rational claims of the community. The afterlife of the kind of agonistic tragedy that *Antigone* represents extends beyond the clash between family and state. Tragedy continually stages the disastrous consequences of the power of the irrational – both love and hate – in the face of the demands and norms of city, state, and community. Overall Greek tragedy itself demonstrates the inability of reason to control the force of passion, whether it is understood to be "demonic," like a virus injected by a vengeful god, or part of a protagonist's *ethos*.

In the case of *Medea*, that force appears to be essential to the protagonist's character, capable of overriding all other concerns. *Medea* enacts the terrifying story of a woman driven to murder by jealous love. A barbarian princess with magical powers, Medea has fled to Corinth with Jason, having slain her own brother and contrived the murder of Jason's uncle Pelias to further Jason's quest. But when they come in exile to Corinth, Jason decides to abandon Medea and take a new wife. So Medea tricks Jason's new wife into wearing a poisoned robe that makes her die in agony, and then she kills her own children to punish Jason. In her final confrontation with Jason, just before she escapes with the dead bodies of her children, Medea tells Jason *he* is responsible for their deaths: "it was your insolence, and your virgin wedding." Jason replies incredulously, "And just for the sake of that you chose to kill them." But Medea retorts, "Is love so small a pain, do you think, for a woman?" (105–6). Passion thus defines Medea and is the fuel for the tragedy. It is passion is that is uniquely hers, but it is also tied to her gender and her identity as a barbarian: it is her double destiny.

In Euripides' *Heracles*, in contrast, the gods are seen to infect the masculine hero with a murderous anger, disrupting all order and meaning. In the first half of the play, Heracles returns – apparently from the dead – to rescue his father Amphitryon, his wife Megara, and his children from death at the hands of the tyrant Lycus. No sooner is he victorious, however, than the goddess Iris emerges over the house with the figure of Madness, bent on the task of accomplishing Hera's revenge against Heracles: "Up, then," commands Iris, "unmarried child of blackest Night, / rouse up, harden that relentless heart / send madness on this man, confound his mind / and make him kill his sons" (90). Chaos and disaster descend on the house as Heracles goes mad and slaughters his children. When he recovers his senses, he is stricken with the most profound shame and is saved only by Theseus' offer of shelter in Athens and the creation of a hero-cult upon his death. Like *Medea*, *Heracles* enacts the inexplicability of human rage. It may erupt from a man or a woman, and whether you imagine it comes from the gods or from the heart of human nature, we appear to be powerless before it.

It was this kind of tragedy that inspired the Romans to re-create Greek tragedy by staging revenge, hatred, ambition, and love. Crafted in outsized rhetoric, these tragedies revel in extreme acts that violate all laws and social norms. We may remember Lucius Anneus Seneca as a philosopher for his emphasis on reason and self-control, but he chose to imitate those Greek tragedies most concerned with transgression, in particular his *Hercules Furens* (an imitation of *Heracles*), *Troades*, *Phoenissae, Medea, Phaedra, Oedipus,* and *Thyestes. Thyestes,* for example, begins with the fury Megaera recounting all the crimes of the house of Tantalus and foretelling that Thyestes, his son, will come to eat his own children. Through a set of artful speeches and choral odes, the play unfolds a series of horrific events driven by Atreus' desire for revenge against his brother Thyestes. When it appears that there will be peace between the two kings, Atreus instead has Thyestes' children killed and cooked, and then served to Thyestes while he is drunk. The play concludes with Atreus' exultation over his crime. As Gordon Braden has observed, in general, "the basic plot of a Senecan play is that of inner passion which bursts upon and desolates an unexpecting and largely uncomprehending world, an enactment of the mind's disruptive power over external reality" (39). There is no conclusion of moral satisfaction; what remains is only the sense that all the worst in human nature has prevailed.

The Renaissance transformations of the tragedy of desire have their roots in Seneca's obsession with the irrational, but they can also explore the power of love denied. In *Romeo and Juliet,* Shakespeare adapts a classical comic theme: the passion of young lovers blocked by parents or society at large, yet brought together in the end in a union that remakes social bonds. He turned this pattern into a story of impulsive young love, inexplicably and unstoppably torn apart by an equally irrational conflict between two warring families. Romeo's obsessive love for Rosalind may be an occasion for laughter at the play's beginning, but his equally impulsive desire for Juliet is not, and they are caught up in a blinding maelstrom of violence that brings them and others down with it. (Of course, Shakespeare also knew how to make fun of such tragedies, as the parody of "Pyramus and Thisby" set in *A Midsummer Night's Dream* suggests.) Later in his career Shakespeare returns to the tragedy of desire on a much grander scale, in *Antony and*

Cleopatra. There, in a spectacular historical landscape, Shakespeare unfolds an intertwined political and love tragedy defined by the conflict of the values of West and East, Rome and Egypt, male and female. While without question the West, and everything embodied in Rome and Caesar, wins, we cannot say which side of the conflict is to be held as better or true. Antony and Cleopatra themselves embody the dissolution of opposites: they constantly exchange roles. As Cleopatra recalls with pleasure, she "put my tires and mantles on him, whilst / I wore his sword Philippan" (2.4.22–3); he plays the woman and she the man. Antony dies by his own hand, in Roman style but in delusion, while Cleopatra dies both as an Egyptian, bitten by the asp of the Nile, and as a Roman, all "marble-constant" (5.2.240).

In general, Shakespeare seems to have preferred political tragedies to love tragedies (while his comedies, especially the dark ones, always skirt the edge of tragedy). The passions of politics, revenge, and power, rather than love, tended to fuel the English Renaissance tragic imagination – but there are notable exceptions. Webster wrote two remarkable tragedies, *The White Devil* and *The Duchess of Malfi*, which have to do with forbidden love. *The White Devil* is darker and more cynical: the love is adulterous lust, conducted in the context of Italian power politics, and no one admires the lovers. In contrast, *The Duchess of Malfi* has at its center an aristocratic widow's passion for her steward, a love forbidden both by convention and by her brother's irrational opposition to her marrying again. Here desire is at once very down to earth and ennobling. Ford's *'Tis Pity She's a Whore* stages the incestuous love of Giovanni and Annabella, which transgresses the line between heroic defiance and darkest sin, where infamy mixes with glory.

While a favorite theme of the commedia in the Spanish Golden Age was also the conflict between honor, duty, and desire, the tragedy of desire had perhaps its most exquisite articulation in the French neoclassical drama, and especially the plays of Corneille and Racine. The core conflict of Corneille's groundbreaking *Le Cid* is the interaction of the passion of love, honor, and allegiance to the family. The play begins with the recognition of a powerful love between Chimène and Rodrigue, which is about to be sealed by marriage until a dispute arises between their fathers, a matter of honor over who is appointed as the prince's tutor. The matter of honor escalates when Rodrigue's father calls upon Rodrigue to revenge his wounded honor, and Rodrigue kills Chimène's father. She is then bound to seek Rodrigue's death even though her love for him never wanes; as she declares to her governess: "I love, Elvira, nay, I worship him. / My passion and my anger are at odds. . . . / Whatever power my love has over me, / I will not shrink from doing what is right. / I go unwavering where my duty calls" (69). The conflict appears irreconcilable until the king forgives Rodrigue because he is a war hero. The dilemma is then resolved by monarchical fiat; only in a world of absolute power can the tragedy of the conflict of love and duty be averted.

Racine's *Phèdre* focuses on the transgressive and destructive power of desire itself. In Euripides' version of this story in his *Hippolytus*, the action is introduced by Aphrodite, who informs the audience that she has infected Queen Phaedra with desire for her stepson, Hippolytus, in revenge for Hippolytus' preferring the life of hunting to the pursuit of women. The story then plays out Phaedra's struggle to contain her desire, until the moment that she confesses, in the mistaken belief that her husband, King Theseus, is dead. Hippolytus spurns her, and when Theseus returns, she tells him in a moment of desperation that Hippolytus raped her. Theseus curses his son, who is killed by Poseidon as he attempts to escape Thebes. Phaedra then poisons herself. In his adaptation of this story, Racine both magnifies and mystifies the power of desire by removing the obvious agency of Aphrodite. As a result, his Phèdre and the audience alike struggle to understand the source of that power that cannot be denied. While Racine is concerned in his preface to the play to state that indeed his play is strictly moral, it cannot be entirely moralized (even if he gives Hippolyte a "flaw" in his love for the young woman Aricie – whom Racine invented – against his father's wishes). The opposition between love and duty that is so artfully knit and forcefully unentangled in *Le Cid* is swallowed up by the flames that consume Phèdre.

While less the focus of Renaissance tragedy, forbidden love and frustrated desire were important themes in Romantic tragedy and melodrama, often intertwined with themes of power and politics. The Romantic hero is caught in a complex web of compulsions and prohibitions. Its inheritance from the tragedy of the previous century is to see desire as in itself fundamentally wrong in social terms; yet that very passion is portrayed as the essence of the heroic and even the human ethos. As Raymond Williams observes, in that case what happens is that the forms of desire become more devious and often perverse, and what looks like revolt is more properly the desperate defiance of heaven and hell. There is a related preoccupation with remorse: deep, pervasive, and beyond all its nominal causes. For in Romantic tragedy man is guilty of the ultimate and nameless crime of being himself. (94)

For these heroes "being oneself" and living as a criminal often involves taking on a different persona or disguise: in that persona they can live out their rebellion, but it is always in tension with their socially defined identity, paradoxically their "true" nature. Thus Hernani's "bandit" self that also loves Doña Sol will eventually come into conflict with his aristocratic self, which holds him to his familial culture of honor. In contrast, in *Ruy Blas*, the hero is a man of low birth and a servant who is filled with ambition and with love for the queen; he is lured into a plot in which, under the disguise of a nobleman, he must betray the queen whom he loves. But once he comes into that role he cannot be both, and he dies having killed the man who would undo his love yet committing suicide because the queen has said that she cannot pardon him. Unregulated and painful desire is the essence of these characters: it fills every word they speak, yet at the same time, it cannot ever be fully expressed.

The tragedy of desire lives on today in films with characters who defy social convention in pursuit of their passion. Some of the most popular films with a tragic theme center on forbidden or doomed love, revealing the power of this kind of tragedy to capture our emotions, especially in a culture more fascinated by sexual desire than political ambition (even *Titanic*, that epic disaster film, plays out a reversal-of-fortune story with a tragedy of forbidden love across class boundaries). Its early roots are in late nineteenth-century melodrama, obsessed with young lovers separated by angry parents or wicked villains (there, of course, the virtuous tend to be rewarded in the end). Going beyond melodrama, film has been effective in exploring the destructive power of desire in a world wrenched apart by war, revolution, or modernization. What is *King Kong*, after all, but a tragedy of desire? On the face of it the situation is absurd: it is about a very large ape's doomed love for a very attractive blonde. But the more compelling part of the story is the way in which that love is played out over Kong's dislocation from the prehistoric savage world of Skull Island to the modern and equally savage world of New York. The tragedy of the story is in the destruction of everything that Kong embodies, which is the mystery of a lost world. *King Kong's* nearly contemporary counterpart is Joseph Von Sternberg's *The Blue Angel* (*Der blaue Engel*). It is a story of a repressed, elderly schoolteacher, Immanuel Rath, who becomes entranced with a cabaret singer, Lola (played by Marlene Dietrich). While Rath first comes to Lola's performances to condemn her, he falls for her and is drawn into a relationship in which she both takes all his money and humiliates him, stripping him of all of his former authority and identity. In this story, traditional authority, status, and morality dissolve through eros, but Rath's decline reflects the dying world that was the Weimar Republic before the rise of Hitler. What distinguishes such tragic films from mere melodrama is this sense that the fate of the lovers is inextricable from our common destiny in an unstable world of shifting values and loyalties.

Tragic Plotlessness

Plot, in the end, defines the perverse satisfaction of tragedy: the pleasure and terror of tragedy lie in the anticipation and experience of the story's shape and end, fearing while knowing, and in the end, being somehow consoled that what appears must be. But we must always remember that these stories are of our own making. What can we learn about the effects of the tragic plot from Samuel Beckett's *Waiting for Godot*, that play that so famously appears to have no plot at all? Is there a reversal, or a change in fortune? Does anything ever change – and does it matter?

Something does happen between the first and second acts, without our witnessing it: the tree grows four or five leaves, and Didi knows (while Gogo cannot remember). When Pozzo and Lucky enter again, something *has* happened: Pozzo is blind. Didi struggles to understand how and why, hectoring Pozzo with repeated questions about time. Pozzo replies, in a rage:

Have you not done tormenting me with your accursed time! It's abominable! When! When! One day, is that not enough for you, one day he went dumb, one day I went blind, one day we'll go deaf, one day we were born, one day we shall die, the same day, the same second, is that not enough for you? *(Calmer.)* They give birth astride of a grave, the light gleams an instant, then it's night once more. *(He jerks the rope.)* On! (103)

Despite Pozzo's protests, it does matter, because the implicit question behind Didi's insistent "when" is "why": the great questions of *why* Lucky is dumb, *why* Pozzo is blind, *why* we must suffer, and *why* we must die.

Something does change over the course of the play in Didi's heart: it is in his passionate desire for change, in his search to find significance in the distinction between yesterday, today, and tomorrow. For Didi, making distinctions of time is connected with memory, and memory is linked, in turn, with meaning. After Pozzo and Lucky exit for the second time, Didi is left with more questions: Is Pozzo really blind? Did he dream it? Did something happen? But while Gogo attends to the pain in his feet and slumbers, Didi wonders:

> Was I sleeping, while the others suffered? Am I sleeping now? Tomorrow, when I wake, or think I do, what shall I say of today? That with Estragon my friend, at this place, until the fall of night, I waited for Godot? That Pozzo passed, with his carrier, and that he spoke to us? Probably. But in all that what truth will there be? *(Estragon, having struggled with his boots in vain, is dozing off again. Vladimir looks at him.)* He'll know nothing. He'll tell me about the blows he received and I'll give him a carrot. *(Pause.)* Astride of a grave and a difficult birth. Down in the hole, lingeringly, the grave-digger puts on the forceps. We have time to grow old. The air is full of our cries. *(He listens.)* But habit is a great deadener. *(He looks again at Estragon.)* At me too someone is looking, of me too someone is saying, he is sleeping, he knows nothing, let him sleep on. *(Pause.)* I can't go on! *(Pause.)* What have I said? (104–5)

The question at the heart of Didi's searching and memory is the significance of suffering, represented in multiple forms. Suffering is evoked in the play in the most basic way in the painfulness of Gogo's foot in an ill-fitting boot (the play's first image), the everyday pain of life. But suffering also lies in Lucky's shouldering of Pozzo's burdens, a suffering that one character inflicts upon another, for no apparent reason other than that it has always been so, and they are inexorably bound together. Suffering also lies in Pozzo's blindness in the second act, prompting Didi's anxious question as to whether it is his obligation to respond: "Let us do something," he cries, "while we have a chance" (90). And most poignantly, Didi suffers himself in moments of aware-ness like this, when he becomes open to the cries in the night. While Godot never comes in the end, we powerfully feel Didi's desire to make meaning out of the pain and to be sensible of the pain, through remembering.

"Astride of a grave and a difficult birth. Down in the hole, linger-ingly, the grave-digger puts on the forceps. We have time to grow old. The air is full of our cries." This final image has a powerful ambiguity as it links birth with death: are we born into death, or is each death the seed of a new life, in the ritual tradition of tragic sacrifice? To call *Waiting for Godot* a tragedy forces us to ask the question of why we want there to be crisis, why we want to see a change. It is in the moment of crisis, through the acts of recognition and remembrance, that we come to grips with suffering, rather than numbly living through every day of our lives.

CHAPTER 4

Tragic Heroes

Is tragedy something that happens only to heroes? If one is asked this question, the prudent reply usually is: "Well, first I need to know what a hero is." From there the conversation can run in circles: tragedy shapes our idea of what a hero is, but then we measure her or him by the values of our time. And tragic heroism is always in tension with these communal beliefs and standards of behavior.

In short, tragic heroes can frighten us. They are defined by conflict and often they are simply not likable. Antigone's stubbornness is terrifying when she resolutely rejects the support of those who love her. While we are led to believe that Hamlet might once have been the most "sweet prince," he spends most of his time abusing his companions and relatives, and he is responsible for at least five deaths (not counting Ophelia's). Romantic heroes like Karl von Moor in Schiller's *The Robbers* or more modern figures like Ibsen's Hedda Gabler may inspire devotion, but they are people with whom it would be impossible to live. Tragic heroes embody both all that we hope for ourselves and all that we fear or hate.

But we do crave their presence. Aristotle has long puzzled readers with the curious statement in his *Poetics* that you can have a tragedy without "characters" but not "without a plot" (Section 10, p. 27). This notion is alien to modern readers who think that tragedy is all about what happens to the main "characters." We can't imagine talking about *King Lear* or *Hedda Gabler* without focusing on the motivation and experience of those individuals. But tragic criticism has not always been fixated on heroes. Classical and neoclassical commentators mostly focused on the formal issues of plot, style, and decorum, not on the agency of the protagonist. It was the Romantic critics, and particularly the Germans, who came to highlight the hero's mind and actions as the core of the tragic experience (see Cave: 152). In *On Aristotle and Greek Tragedy* John Jones chides critics for not being able to see that Aristotle's "change of fortune" does not require "the heroic, suffering solitary who is supposed to stand at the center of the stage, like Hamlet" (14).

This chapter explores the challenges tragic heroes pose to understanding both the plays and the cultures that produced them. Tragic heroes can be categorized into a series of types: the tyrant, the rebel, the warrior, the lover, the martyr – with many shadings among them. Any effort at taxonomy soon demonstrates that it is very difficult to draw a line between these types: for example, the lover can become a kind of tyrant, the rebel may also be a martyr, and it often becomes hard to distinguish between the tyrant and the rebel who defies him. The various types of tragic heroes are expressed differently in the evolution of the genre, and, in particular, when class and gender play a role.

Hamartia

Perhaps no idea has gripped the conversation about tragic heroism more than the "tragic flaw." Like a conscientious doctor, we poke and prod each protagonist to find the "flaw" or the vulnerability that explains everything. The *American Heritage Dictionary* confidently defines the tragic flaw as "a flaw in the character of the protagonist of a tragedy that brings the protagonist to ruin or sorrow." In contemplating the difference between Greek and Christian tragedy, W. H. Auden readily concurred with the idea that the Greek hero's "flaw" was instrumental in the hero's downfall, not necessarily because a flaw creates the tragic situation, but because that disaster is "sent him by the gods as a punishment for having such a flaw" (1). In defining the heroism of the modern "common man," Arthur Miller still couldn't get away from the idea of the tragic flaw, even while he tried to shape it into a virtue:

> The flaw, or crack in the character, is really nothing – and need be nothing, but his inherent unwillingness to remain passive in the face of

what he conceives to be a challenge to his dignity, his image of his right-
ful status. Only the passive, only those who accept their lot without
active retaliation, are "flawless." (1949)

Even if the flaw is thus construed positively, it is still understood as
part of the hero's ethos, not as an action or error.

The compulsion to find the hero's "flaw" surely has to do with our
desperate need to find the cause of the tragic catastrophe. We want to
know why these terrible events have been visited upon this person
(and we hope they are not visited on us). We do not want our tragic
heroes to be villains, tediously deserving of punishment, but we do
not want them to be perfect either. Aristotle specified what he thought
was the right course in shaping the tragic hero: the proper tragic hero
"is the man who is neither a paragon of virtue and justice nor under-
goes the change to misfortune through any real badness or wickedness
but because of some mistake (*hamartia*)" (38, 1453a10). As they do
with so many elements of Aristotle's text, generations of readers have
tried to puzzle out what he meant. What's the difference between
wickedness and *hamartia*? In Greek, *hamartia* means most literally a
"missing of a mark" (as in archery or spear-throwing). A strict reading
of the text would construe *hamartia* as a "mistake" or an "error of
judgment" unconnected to the character's moral condition. However,
since the Middle Ages critics have tended to translate this word as a
"moral fault or shortcoming" (Jones: 15). The distinction is a crucial
one. Even the best of us makes mistakes, but a moral flaw is particular
to an individual and part of his or her nature. As the horrified audience witnesses the consequences of the hero's *hamartia*, it may be a
consolation to say, "I am not like that, or I can try not to be like that;
if so, surely this misfortune will not happen to me." But in the end,
the notion of the "tragic flaw" is not a helpful critical tool for understanding the tragic hero. It obscures the complexity of the relationship
between the hero's values and those of the world he or she inhabits.

Instead of assuming the hero's moral character, in contrast you
could see him or her as the ritual scapegoat, a victim who takes on
the collective guilt or pollution of society. With the death or expulsion
of that scapegoat, a society is thought to be cleansed of its evils. As
René Girard describes the scenario in *Violence and the Sacred*:

> The surrogate victim dies so that the entire community, threatened by
> the same fate, can be reborn in a new or renewed cultural order. Having

sown the seeds of death, the god, ancestor, or mythic hero then dies
himself or selects a victim to die in his stead. In so doing he bestows
new life on men. (255)

The scapegoat takes on the collective guilt, not necessarily because he
or she is guilty of any particular crime or sin or has a flaw, but rather
because *someone* must do so. Tragedy certainly features characters represented as innocent victims who – willingly or not – are sacrificed to
heal the *polis*. So, in Euripides' plays, Iphigenia must be killed in order
for the Greek ships to find the wind to sail to Troy in *Iphigenia in Aulis,*
or Polyxena must die in *Hecuba*. But, as Girard argues, one could also
see Oedipus as a scapegoat or sacrificial victim who must be expelled
from Thebes, not because he is proud or defies the gods, but because
someone must carry that burden to cure the city of the plague of its
cycle of violence.

This association of heroism with sacrifice is intelligible in a Christian
context through the image of Christ as a hero. In this model, the hero
becomes a martyr, again, not because he has a flaw, but as a witness to
his or her faith, and because all of humanity will be saved by that self-
sacrifice. At the end of Milton's *Paradise Lost*, Adam learns what is the
highest form of heroism: "that suffering for Truth's sake / Is fortitude to
highest victory / And to the faithful Death and Gate of Life; / Taught this
by his example whom I now / Acknowledge my Redeemer ever blest"
(XII, 569–73). Such tragic heroism can carry it own dangers. In T. S.
Eliot's *Murder in the Cathedral*, Thomas Becket is visited by four tempters:
the first three, who represent earthly pleasures, priestly power, and
temporal power, are easily countered, but Becket does not expect the
fourth temptation, which is to see "eternal grandeur" in martyrdom
(39). Becket must find a way to submit to sacrifice without pride or to
act without will, learning that "acting is suffering, and suffering action"
(40). His death, both as an imitation of the death of Christ and as a ritual
sacrifice that renews the land, poses the critical problem of heroism in
martyrdom: can an act be heroic without will or agency?

To act or to suffer: in the end, it can be very difficult to disentangle
the elements of choice, agency, and suffering in the depiction of the
tragic hero. The paradox that tragic heroism poses is that to assert
yourself is to destroy yourself. And has the tragic hero truly chosen to
do so, or is he or she compelled, a victim of circumstances, social conditions, or destiny, pure and simple?

Overreaching

Stay out of trouble, keep a low profile: that's the advice that the Greek chorus usually gives, and the advice that the protagonist must ignore in order to be a hero. The closing lines of *Antigone*'s chorus solemnly declares that "Wisdom is by far the greatest part of joy, / and reverence towards the gods must be safeguarded. / The mighty words of the proud are paid in full / with mighty blows of fate, and at long last / those blows will teach us wisdom" (128). They fear *hubris*, a confidence that goes beyond a strong sense of self to threaten the fabric of ordinary society and the restraints of religion. The chorus of *Murder in the Cathedral* has a less self-serving version of what it means *not* be a hero: "We have suffered various oppression, / But mostly we are left to our own devices, / And we are content if we are left alone. / We try to keep our households in order" (12).

If the watchword of Athenian culture was *mēdē agan*, or "nothing too much," the tragic hero is always "too much": too virtuous, too much in love, too powerful, too angry, too devoted, too reverent, or too intelligent. Aristotle was not a very perceptive judge when it came to this aspect of tragic character, when he insisted that tragic characters "be good" according to social type, and that they be "appropriate; for it is possible for a character to be brave, yet it is not fitting for a woman" (43, 1454a20). Most often the tragic hero acts *inappropriately* in his or her single-minded pursuit of one idea, passion, or mode of action. We admire Oedipus' pursuit of the truth, but we can feel he goes too far. Pentheus is doing his job in protecting his city from the invasion of the bacchants, but he acts too harshly. Even if you allow for the Greek stereotype that women are prone to deception, lust, and irrationality in general, Clytemnestra, Medea, Agave, Antigone, Cleopatra, Lady Macbeth, and Joan of Arc are heroines whose behavior is entirely inappropriate to the type of womanhood – and that is the point. These are characters whose actions go beyond what is expected, whether you believe that they are acting out of their *ethos* or seized by *daimon*.

Bernard Knox argued in *The Heroic Temper* that Sophocles invented "the presentation of the tragic dilemma in the figure of a single dominating character," a character who often seems insanely unreasonable and loyal only to her or his own self-conception (1). While Aeschylean tragedy is filled with characters of this type (for example, Prometheus or Eteocles in *Seven against Thebes*), one must acknowledge that Sophocles' lineup of intransigent characters is intimidating: witness Philoctetes, Ajax, Antigone, Creon, Electra, Oedipus, even Heracles in his torment at the end of *The Women of Trachis*. Through the chorus's ambivalent responses, Sophocles manages to generate admiration and sympathy for these characters, even though they – and we – recoil from them. Their power evokes the Greek phenomenon of the hero cult, the ritual practice of honoring the dead who have distinguished themselves by some remarkable deed, good or evil. Such figures were understood to be inherently powerful, however terrible (54–8).

It is at first puzzling that a culture that so prized democracy, reason, and loyalty to the city would so obsessively display to itself the defiance and transgressions of such individuals. The easy explanation is that tragedy was meant to be a cautionary tale. By this conventional account, tragedy should demonstrate the consequences of such outrageous behavior and thus affirm the values of moderation and civic obedience. If this were so, however, why is the hero loved as much as he or she is shunned? "Oedipus Tyrannus" is also "Oedipus the King," at once the savior of the city and its enemy, both obviously and covertly. He might have saved the city through solving the riddle of the Sphinx, but he also embodies the pollution of violence and incest. As Vernant observes, it is by staging such strong characters that "the world of the city is called into question and its fundamental values are challenged in the ensuing debate" (9). Tragedy poses problems, not solutions or lessons, in the contest between individual excess and communal needs.

Later re-creations of tragedy will return to this type as the model for tragic heroism as a form of exceptionalism, for better or worse. In later versions of this type, the tragic hero can take many forms: the tyrant, the rebel, or what Eugene Waith called the "Herculean hero," identified with both godlike strength in the service of mankind and towering rage. All of these characters who burst social and communal constraints reach beyond what defines the human, and in that space the distinctions between them begin to blur. For example, in *Antigone*, Creon, the king who is revealed as a tyrant, and Antigone, his nemesis, are uncomfortably alike. When Creon is introduced, he seems like the chorus's ally and the supreme Periclean man, ready to sacrifice all for the public welfare, whereas Antigone appears entirely alone and compelled only by her own desire to face down Creon. However, it takes Creon to enforce Antigone's isolation, for she is not alone when she gains the support of Ismene, Haemon, and the chorus, whereas Creon becomes cut off when he grasps for godlike power. In the end, Creon does change his mind, responding to the chorus's advice. This act, which is too late, paradoxically saves him from the name of tyrant yet disqualifies him (at least for some) from being a tragic hero. He is broken, having lost his identity and agency. Antigone, in contrast, while she calls herself a martyr, hardly seems like a victim. She remains true to her defiance and thus consistent in character to the end.

Greek tragedy typically pairs the rebel and the tyrant hero thus to define each other and to break down the boundary between them. Aeschylus' *Prometheus Bound* opposes Prometheus, the titan who stole the gift of fire, against Zeus, who is determined to punish him for this act. While Zeus himself never appears on stage, he is represented by the uncompromising figures of Might and Violence, images of Zeus' tyranny. At the same time, we are reminded that Zeus himself came to power through an act of rebellion against his own father Kronos: the new ruler of the gods has brought in new "customs that have no law to them" (144). Thus, rebellion and tyranny call for the same character defying the existing order. In *The Bacchae*, Dionysus comes to Thebes as an outsider, inciting the women to abandon their responsibilities and to flock to the hills to live as maenads. Pentheus is the angry young king who wants to suppress this new movement that looks like liberation. Yet Dionysus is a god, and Pentheus a mere mortal, and his actions are interpreted as a resistance to the god's will. Pentheus is thus the upstart, and is punished for his bold defiance. Who, then, in these plays is the rebel, and who is the tyrant? Tyranny itself is a kind of transgression that produces rebellion and martyrdom, in a strong symbiosis.

The plays of Seneca transmitted the type of the tyrant/rebel hero to later generations of playwrights, especially to the Renaissance. In Seneca's hands, the superhuman hero became subhuman. Roman history itself produced spectacular tyrants like Nero and Caligula, and in the context of this world Seneca fashioned the Greek images into full-blown tyrant heroes like Atreus of *Thyestes* or Lycus of *Hercules Furens*. Lacking the ambivalent nature of Sophocles' Oedipus or Creon, Seneca's tyrants are terrifying machines of desire who consume everything in their path: they are racked with passion, whether it is sexual desire or a lust for revenge. When classical tragedy was reborn in the mid-fifteenth century, it was through Seneca: the first neoclassical play, Albertino Mussato's *Ecerinis* (ca. 1315) represented the recent tyranny of Ezzelino III in a way that was meant as a warning to the present rulers of Padua (see pp. 108–9). The first Italian Senecan tragedy, Giambattista Giraldi Cinthio's *Orbecche* (1541), features violence, cannibalism, and incest as heroic action. It was through such plays that the image of tragic heroism was revived in Europe (see Braden).

English writers drew on this inheritance from Seneca to fashion their own versions of the hero who "overreaches," either as rebel or tyrant. The vernacular English stage had seen two types of tyrant figures: the miracle play's blustering Herod and the morality play's overweening kings like Thomas Preston's Cambyses (see Bushnell, 1990: ch. 3). Interweaving these precedents with Senecan conventions, Shakespeare fashioned Richard III into the first full-blown tyrannical protagonist to stride the English stage. Richard plows his way through a series of secret crimes, while seducing almost everyone he encounters, until he can disguise his villainy no longer, and the tide turns against him. Far from being wracked with guilt, Richard takes pleasure in what he does, and through his soliloquies we are implicitly asked to admire his overreaching as he plays "the devil" (1.3.344). The audience is manipulated to be both fascinated and repelled by his ascent, while the attractions of Richmond, the "proper" king, pale in comparison.

When he used the term "overreacher" to describe Christopher Marlowe's heroes, Harry Levin identified in these characters a common strain:

> His protagonist is never Everyman but always "l'uomo singolare," the exceptional man who becomes king because he is a hero, not hero because he is a king; the private individual who remains captain of his fate, at least until his ambition overleaps itself; the overreacher whose tragedy is more an action than a passion, rather an assertion of man's will than an acceptance of God's. (1952: 24)

These overreachers are simultaneously tyrants and rebels, when they seek to impose their will on everyone else, defying convention, existing power structures, and even the laws of nature. With the exception of *Edward II*, Marlowe's heroes are never sacrificial victims, while they resolutely chart their own paths of exceptional – and mostly criminal – behavior. Over the course of two plays, Tamburlaine blazes a path of destruction across several continents. In a series of formulaic scenes, he arrives in a city, declares with a great flourish his intent to conquer his adversaries, meets with resistance, and then overcomes his enemies. The reader would have to work hard to believe that Marlowe intended us to see Tamburlaine's death at the end of the second play as the result of some "flaw" or even a punishment for hubris. Rather the doctor who examines his dying body pronounces that he has simply burned himself out. Faustus and Barabas of *The Jew of Malta* also determine their own paths of ascent and destruction: Faustus in his search for knowledge and power, and Barabas in his avarice and desire for revenge. Barabas never repents, nor does Faustus, even though his good angel calls on him to do so.

The heirs of the Marlovian overreachers are the extreme heroes of Jacobean tragedy, who shock us in their boundless desire for power, revenge, or sex. While it may take them some time to get there, they end by glorifying their excesses: who can forget the spectacle of the incestuous Giovanni in *'Tis Pity She's A Whore* (1633), in his final moment, entering with his beloved sister's heart impaled on his dagger? In *The Revenger's Tragedy* (1607), each character seems to try to outdo the other in evil, while they undo themselves; there, the main avenger character Vindice himself might have escaped without punishment except he cannot resist boasting of his "witty" revenge.

In contrast, Macbeth, Coriolanus, and Antony are cast from the mold of the "Herculean" warrior hero, whose supreme masculinity produces disaster rather than good for the state. As in the case of Heracles, the hero's prowess in war brings him into a position of power, then dooms him. All that makes him admired as a warrior breaks him as a ruler. Martial and masculine values are further challenged, when we see each hero dominated by a powerful woman who both demands that he "be a man" and undermines him. Macbeth comes to royal favor because of his violence in service to the state and then is compelled by the witches and Lady Macbeth to grasp the throne. Once Macbeth is king, his desperation to maintain his primacy and masculinity defines his tyranny and defeats him. Antony, too, is the preeminent warrior, "the garland of the war" (4.15.77). In Cleopatra's imagination, while he lived, "His legs bestrid the ocean: his reared arm / Crested the world" (5.2.102–3). But in the play, he is only remarkable in the excess of his passion for Cleopatra, the antithesis and the complement of the warrior's ardor. Coriolanus is also treated as if he is semi-divine: as Comenius describes his leadership of his troops, "he is their god; he leads them like a thing / Made by some other deity than Nature" (4.6.90–1). But all that makes him a god at war makes him a political disaster in the republic of Rome. In that world he appears "insolent, / O'ercome with pride, ambitious past all thinking, / Self-loving" (4.6.30–2) and disdainful the Roman citizens whom he calls curs (see Waith: ch. 5). Unlike the "overreacher" hero, in that sense, the Herculean hero does become a victim of his own actions, not because his aggression and masculinity are necessarily wrong, but because they become warped or displaced.

As English Renaissance tragedy dwindled into the moralism of a later century, the heroes of excess became increasingly diminished, and he or she was never allowed to escape unscathed. Most of the heroes of bourgeois and eighteenth-century tragedy are neither very attractive nor even very interesting. French neoclassical tragedy does feature single-minded and even extremist heroes, but even then the authors were careful to create an economy of character in which that excess of vice is tempered for more delicate sensibilities, and virtue itself always has a strand of weakness that allows for a disastrous end. Racine is careful to point out that his Phèdre is not a monster, because he tried hard "to make her slightly less odious than in the tragedies of the ancients" (145). Even the Néron of his *Britannicus* is not the full-blown tyrant Nero, but rather a nascent one, still troubled by moral concerns: "in a word, he is here a budding monster, but one who does not dare yet to declare himself, and who seeks to color his wicked actions" (63). The heroes of Corneille and Racine are ultimately bound by the decorum of their society, even as they strain against it.

It remained for Romantic tragedy to reinvent the "overreacher" hero. Victor Hugo's *Hernani* created a scandal in 1827 not only because it violates formal rules, but also because the characters are (to use William Howarth's terms) both sublime and grotesque in their villainy and extremity of passion. All the characters of *Hernani* go too far: Hernani and the old Don Ruy Gomez both adore Doña Sol and are obsessed with revenge; the king Don Carlos also loves Doña Sol while he craves imperial power, and Doña Sol herself single-mindedly pursues her passion for Hernani. We are led to believe that a happy ending could come out of a moderation of these desires, when Don Carlos offers Hernani clemency in an effort to establish his own new identity as emperor (and everyone discovers that Hernani is not a bandit but really an aristocrat). However, passion triumphs when Ruy Gomez appears to claim Hernani's life. The play ends in the suicides of Doña Sol, Hernani, and finally Ruy Gomez himself. The tyranny of love and honor dooms all.

Romantic tragedy also revived political drama, if always with a mix of love intermixed with ambition. Schiller's first spectacular Romantic drama, *The Robbers* (1780), features the quintessential rebel hero, Karl von Moor. Like Hernani, Moor is a nobleman turned bandit, rebelling because his father disowned him. In his outlaw life, he expresses the spirit of freedom and anti-aristocratic values, as he robs from the rich to give to the poor, yet at the same time he knows he is contaminated by the crimes and murders that his robber band commits. In the forest, he says, "you step beyond the bounds of humanity – you must either be more than a man, or you are a devil" (103). At the play's end, even though he is in a position to be restored to his long-lost love Amalia and regain his birthright, he refuses and murders Amalia before she can kill herself. He then hands himself over to the law, mocking himself for supposing that he "could make the world a fairer place through terror." But even as he does so he believes in his own power, boasting that "two men such as I would destroy the whole moral order of creation" (159). In its own time, indeed, Schiller's play had a powerful impact, when it was interpreted as a call to rally against tyranny.

Among the modern heirs of the overreacher hero are the gangsters of the modern cinema, in films like *Scarface, Little Caesar, Public Enemy*, and *Bonnie and Clyde*. The gangster hero knows only an existence through violence. In his essay "The Gangster as Tragic Hero," Robert Warshow suggests that in such films the gangster's "brutality itself becomes at once the means to success and the content of success – a success that is defined in its most general terms, not as accomplishment or specific gain, but simply as the unlimited possibility of aggression" (132). That explosion into violence is at once a defiance of social norms and self-expression, the modern version of a tyranny at the margins of society. In *Key Largo*, when asked what he truly wants, the gangster Johnny Rocco only knows that he wants "more." It doesn't matter more of what; he simply needs to grab. The backdrop to the story of

Tony Camonte in Howard Hawks's 1932 version of *Scarface* is a cheap, flashing electric sign, signifying "The World is Yours" (which ironically illuminates the scene of Camonte's bullet-riddled body lying in the gutter at the film's end). And at the climax of *White Heat*, when Cody Jarrett is about to be incinerated in an explosion, he crows triumphantly "Made it, Ma! Top of the world!" The gangster hero must be punished, because he is the tyrant in his own world and an outlaw to the rest, but he also has a presence and a glamour that hold him at the film's center. The contemporary audience's fascination with the gangster hero is powerful testimony to the longevity of the type of the "overreacher" tragic hero, in a modern and rationalist society.

Tragic Women

The Athenian culture of moderation and communal values that produced such overreacher heroes also created memorable tragic women, a remarkable achievement for a culture in which women were meant to be invisible. Greek tragedy happened in public in every sense: the theater was open, and while the events of tragedy might spring from private crises, they were always presented as being enacted publicly. But Athenian women belonged inside, in the service of their families, husband, and children. As Macaria says in *Heracleidae*: "I know a woman should be quiet and / Discreet, and that her place is in the home," but in the next line she declares that she still needs to emerge into the public space, to speak (476–8; see Murnaghan).

Indeed, tragic women are rarely silent, and when they are, it is almost always a sign of danger. Not only do they speak out, but they also commit horrific acts of violence, against themselves and others, whether intentionally or unintentionally. Greek tragedy set the precedent for women to be tragic heroes, both defined by and in defiance of the societal roles they were meant to play. Even more so than their male counterparts, women overreach, because the boundaries drawn for them are more constricting. It is even harder to separate these tragic women into heroic types – into oppressor and martyr, revenger and victim, tyrant and rebel – because the worlds they inhabit encase them in such contradictory values and expectations. (On Athenian tragic women, see Murnaghan and Zeitlin; on Renaissance tragic women, see Belsey and Rackin.)

Even now, audiences are astounded by the figure of Clytemnestra in the *Oresteia*. She dominates the stage throughout *Agamemnon*, weaving her net of deceit to capture and murder her husband and her king. From her first speech the male chorus is moved to praise her authority, acknowledging that what she has pronounced is "spoken like a man . . . loyal, / full of self-command" (116). At the same time, she also expertly manipulates her femininity, playing the obsequious wife to entrap Agamemnon. She is the female weaver, while she also wields a weapon like a man. Clytemnestra both violates the traditional idea of Greek womanhood and embodies all the darkness of women, stained with blood. The same chorus who praised her even rule at the play's beginning recoils in horror at the end, calling her "mad with ambition / shrilling pride! – some Fury / crazed with carnage rages through your brain – / I can see the flecks of blood inflame your eyes!" (163). In *The Libation Bearers*, this terrifying creature is tamed, renamed as the mother and Orestes' victim, whose act of violence against her husband must be avenged. She does live on in spirit in *The Eumenides*, in the presence of the Furies, the hideous female demons who pursue Orestes to punish his matricide. But they too are appeased by the intervention of the goddess Athena and the institution of the Athenian court of law. The effect of the entire trilogy is to contain this kind of feminine power in the context of a narrative in which vengeance gives way to law (see Zeitlin: 87–119).

Women often take on the roles of tragic plotter and revenger, in the mode of Clytemnestra, weaving a net to entrap those who have wronged them or to garner power for themselves or their husbands or children. These women are driven to be "man-like" but also fueled by a passion that is seen as specifically feminine. Medea is perhaps the most notable example of the tragic heroine whose single-minded passion grants her a power in the play that no one can resist. She and Clytemnestra prefigure later strong tragic heroes who act without mercy in defense of their children, parents, or husband, or to advance their cause. Tamora, Queen of the Goths in Shakespeare's *Titus Andronicus*, is an early, lurid example. Lady Macbeth is a more complex version, because she presents her own scheming for her husband's ascent to the throne as a violation of her femininity, so much that she must call to the "spirits that tend on moral thoughts" to "unsex me here. / And fill me from the crown to the toe topful /Of direst cruelty!" (1.5.40–3). At the same time her ambition and "mettle" are consistent with the tradition of the tragic heroine that maneuvers for her man.

At the same time, however, while such characters may position the tragic hero as the aggressor, they are also characteristically the victim. After all, Medea's self-defense that she acts because Jason has wounded her suggests that she sees herself as a victim, and she is given a long speech in which she bemoans the oppressive fate of women. Tragedy does indeed dwell obsessively on the image of the woman as victim. Euripides' *The Trojan Women* painfully depicts the effects of the Trojan War on the women of the conquered city. Step by step, the women's fates are revealed: slavery, concubinage, and death. Women here can only glory in their traditional role of lamentation, the one powerful kind of speech they were granted in Greek society (Murnaghan: 11). In a different way, Euripides' *Iphigenia in Aulis* makes the status of victim heroic: Iphigenia first resists her father's plan to sacrifice her, in order to bring on the winds to blow the Greeks toward Troy, but then she embraces that role, a surrender admired by all except her desperate and enraged mother Clytemnestra. (Surviving texts do include an ending, thought to be a later interpolation, in which a messenger reports that Iphigenia is miraculously saved at the last minute by a hind substituted in her place; most modern translators omit it as "untragic.") Shakespeare's Desdemona also looks mostly like a victim, when we see her character relentlessly blackened by Iago, and she is caught up in his web of deceit, finally dying passively as Othello smothers her in their bed.

But the case of Desdemona reminds us of the difficulty in separating the image of female victim from the transgressor. After all, Desdemona did commit an act of defiance, in eloping with Othello and thus betraying her father. In some cases the woman commits a horrific act in ignorance, or because she is possessed. Deianeira in *The Women of Trachis* murders her husband Heracles, but she does so unwittingly, giving him a poisoned robe that she believes is a love charm. Like the rest of the women of Thebes in *The Bacchae*, Agave is driven by Dionysus to flee madly into the hills to live a maenad's life, but it is she whom Dionysus punishes most horribly for her "impiety," for in her madness, she rips apart the body of her own son Pentheus with her bare hands. In one of the most terrifying images in Greek tragedy, Agave enters the stage, like a warrior, boasting of her kill of a lion while brandishing the severed head of her son. In *Antigone*, Creon creates a situation in which, in order to fulfill her traditionally female role of honoring her dead brother, Antigone must become "unwomanly" and defy his order. Creon sees her act as a challenge to his own masculinity: "I am not the man, not now: she is the man / if this victory goes to her and she goes free" (83). Antigone presents herself as a victim of his outrages even as she asserts her agency and right to act for the good of the city, asking the chorus to look at her as "the last of a great line of kings, / I alone, see what I suffer now / at the hands of what breed of men – / all for reverence, my reverence for the gods" (107). She may hang herself, but she does so to frustrate Creon's plan to condemn her to a living death, walled up alive and alone.

Like Antigone, Cordelia can be seen as a victim of a tyrant who has put her into an impossible situation, but in that role, she becomes a warrior on behalf of the truth, a rebel against her father who wants her to conform to his desires. Cordelia seems the opposite of her sisters, Goneril and Regan, who are cut from the cloth of the woman who "manoeuvres like a man" (*Oresteia*: 103). Impelled by ambition and then by lust for Edmund, the two evil sisters relentlessly scheme their way to seize power, and they are fueled by their desire. But Cordelia's story is more complex. In this world where true love is expressed through defiance of irrational authority, Cordelia's rebellion against tyranny becomes obedience. Thus she can remain the "good woman" while doing all the things that good women should never do, first defying her father and then leading an army to fight her wicked sisters. A Christian woman in this pre-Christian world, she is forgiving and gentle. As Lear comments, in his madness, when she lies dead, her voice still: "Her voice was ever soft, / Gentle, and low, an excellent thing in woman" (5.3.273–4). Simultaneously rebel and good girl, she is sacrificed at the end, but for no reason.

Tragic women who live and die for love can also be seen as acting out another kind of stereotype of femininity. The other side of undying and uncompromising female devotion is unstoppable desire, beyond social norms and its own kind of overreaching. This kind of desire defines a kind of self-expression and self-assertion for women in tragedy, when that love violates social norms. Cleopatra is the queen of Egypt, but we hardly see her ruling. Rather, her strength and her weakness are defined by the power of her love for Antony and her expression of it. Unlike the case for Antony, her desire does not conflict with her majesty; it is her essence. John Webster's Duchess of

Malfi's heroism springs from her simple wish to marry her steward, in contradiction of her brothers' obsession with keeping her a widow. In the context of their persecution, her pure womanliness, expressed in her pregnant body and maternal compunction, constitute her defiance. She is a hero because she wants what any woman might want, and for this she must die.

The emphasis in neoclassical drama on the conflict between love and honor carves out a place for the representation of a woman obsessed with love, even when it is frustrated. Few of these women are pale, wasting victims. Most are striking in their absolute conviction and willfulness. Chimène in *Le Cid* is strong both in her love for Roderige and in her desire for vengeance for her father's death: neither can permit any compromise. Similarly, Émilie in Corneille's *Cinna* fiercely pursues her revenge against Augustus, who was responsible for her father's death. She is in love with Cinna but forces him to express his love by killing Augustus. When the plot is discovered both lovers declare they will kill themselves, but Augustus pardons them and creates the happy ending (much in the same way that the conflicts at the end of *Le Cid* are resolved by the monarch's edict).

Corneille's tragic women achieve their desires almost in spite of themselves (at least in these two plays); Racine's tragic heroines, in contrast, are never allowed to see their desires fulfilled. Phèdre is portrayed as both a victim and an aggressor. According to the playwright, she "is neither entirely guilty nor altogether innocent" (145). Her passion is a punishment given by the gods (though we never see a god on stage to declare it), and she is doomed for the act of speaking her desire. In Racine's *Britannicus*, Junia flees to the temple of the vestal virgins to avoid the lust of Nero after the death of her beloved Britannicus, and in *Bérénice* the heroine is denied the love of Antiochus, who must serve Rome. Even when they do not die, Racine's women are trapped, neither allowed to love nor freed by death.

Racine's and Corneille's women are reborn, with a difference, in the heroines of Romantic drama, who can be at once "damsels in distress," victims of a repressive aristocratic society that traffics in women, and rebels who are the match for the male heroes of the plays. Victor Hugo's heroines, Doña Sol of *Hernani*, Lucretia Borgia of the play of the same name, and the Queen of Spain in *Ruy Blas*, struggle to possess or protect the men they love: Doña Sol, ready to sacrifice all to follow Hernani; Lucretia, the victim of rape and familial depravity, reaching

out to the son who does not know her; and the Queen of Spain, the object of Ruy Blas's desire and a pawn in a game to entrap him. In some ways these tragic heroines are more knowing and more self-possessed than their male counterparts, yet there is no question that their role is as much as an object as it is as a subject. Friedrich Schiller's tragic women, including Amalia of *The Robbers* and Maria Stuart, are defined by their suffering, but it is a suffering that is, in Schiller's view, designed to express the tragic sublime. Their pain at the hands of others elevates them even as it oppresses them.

When Ibsen created his tragic woman, it coincided with a social movement that argued that the fate of women might be different. *A Doll's House* and *Hedda Gabler* both underscore the possibilities, although the plays have opposite trajectories: Nora appears the timid, conventional wife, whereas our first impression of Hedda is that she is a strong, rebellious character, dismissive of bourgeois conventions and willing to play with fire and with her father's pistols, symbols of male power. However, it turns out quite otherwise: Nora is the one who summons up the courage to walk away from her role as wife and mother, whereas Hedda confesses that she is afraid of scandal. For her, the only way out is suicide, whereas Nora contemplates suicide but then takes the harder road. George Bernard Shaw wrote hyperbolically of that act that "Nora's revolt is the end of a chapter of human history. The slam of the door behind her is more momentous than the cannons of Waterloo or Sedan, because when she comes back, it will not be to the old home" (131). Hedda's suicide, in contrast, does cause a scandal (in Judge Brack's last astonished words, "people don't *do* such things"[304]) but life will go on as it did before in that house, only this time with a woman who will play the proper role.

The challenge for contemporary tragedy is to define what it means to be a tragic woman in a world where women *do* have choices: when, like Nora, they *can* walk out the door. The dramatic films of the 1940s and 1950s, in particular, are obsessed with the image of women finding their way in a new society. Some are gangsters' molls and the "fatal women" of film noir; they can use a gun, but, in the end, they always seem to have it used against them. Others are women who may seek to find their own way in the world, or who do not conform and are then forced to make choices. Bette Davis and Joan Crawford are best known for their image of strong women who still are caught in the dilemmas that society forces on them. Davis's Stella Dallas must give up her daughter to see her succeed, because she recognizes that her own class position will hold her daughter back. Crawford's Mildred Pierce is a divorcee who has to go into business to support her two daughters: ironically, her tragedy is driven by the ambition and greed of her elder daughter Veda. In her unending effort to satisfy Veda, Mildred hurtles toward a final confrontation that leads to murder.

Comic as well as tragic films of the post-World-War II period increasingly constrain the choices for women, in contrast to images of strong women from previous decades. These postwar films tend to repeat the old story that women are doomed either to self-sacrifice or to self-destruction. Women in tragedy as opposed to comedy are thus constrained by a kind of double destiny: the destiny of what it means to be a woman in a repressive society and the destiny that is the plot of the play. There is little escape without the intervention of god or king. Some choose death, as both an escape and a form of self-assertion. As Nicole Loraux observes so eloquently in *Tragic Ways of Killing a Woman*, "the woman in tragedy is more entitled to play the man in her death than the man is to assume any aspect of woman's conduct, even in his manner of death. For women there is liberty in tragedy – liberty in death" (17). This is a brutal message to send, that the only means to liberty and mastery is suicide. For the male tragic hero, suicide or death is often the fulfillment of a life of self-assertion but for the female tragic hero, it may be an end in itself.

Tragedy and the Common Man

In 1949 Arthur Miller delivered a manifesto on "Tragedy and the Common Man," in defense of the possibility of tragedy in a modern world in which we all seem more or less "common":

> In this age few tragedies are written. It has often been held that the lack is due to a paucity of heroes among us, or else that modern man has had the blood drawn out of his organs of belief by the skepticism of science, and the heroic attack on life cannot feed on an attitude of reserve and circumspection. For one reason or another, we are often held to be below tragedy – or tragedy above us. The inevitable conclusion is, of course, that the tragic mode is archaic, fit only for the very highly placed, the kings or the kingly, and where this admission is not

made in so many words it is most often implied. I believe that the common man is as apt a subject for tragedy in its highest sense as kings were. (1)

To be common, in this sense, is to be ordinary, not extraordinary, in terms of both life experience and rank or class. The idea that tragedy can only happen to kings or queens goes back to Aristotle's observation that tragic protagonists not only tend to fall between the extremes of virtue and vice but also that they were "those who stand in great repute and prosperity, like Oedipus and Thyestes: conspicuous men from families of that kind" (38, 1453a10). The tragedies he knew did indeed feature the lives of famous warriors and royalty, gods and goddesses. Citizens, slaves, watchmen, soldiers, guards, and nurses are mostly nameless, whether in the corporate chorus or as individual actors. In some cases, like the nurse in Euripides' *Hippolytus*, they can influence the action, and in others they are featured in single episodes (like the sentry in *Antigone*), but most often they act to show how they are most distinctly not heroic. As that sentry confesses when he hands over Antigone to Creon, "It's pure joy to escape the worst yourself, / it hurts a man to bring down his friends. / But all that, I'm afraid means less to me / than my own skin. That's the way I am made (81).

But despite what Miller suggests, even the Greeks could begin to see tragedy in the ordinary, and for centuries playwrights have experimented with the notion of the "tragedy of the common man." In Aristophanes' *Frogs*, Aeschylus makes fun of Euripides for giving a voice to all his characters, slaves as well as mistresses, but Euripides proudly defends that choice: "I staged," he boasts, "the life of everyday, the way we live" (62). It is true that with the reinvention of tragedy in the Renaissance as the fall of those in "high estate," little scope was left for the idea that tragedy could be something that happens to ordinary people. When such people do appear in these plays, they often serve as the counterpoint to the protagonist's suffering. With notable exceptions, like the anonymous servant in *King Lear*, who rises up to fight Cornwall when he tortures Gloucester, or the servants of Cleopatra who join her in death, the common folk and citizens of Shakespearean tragedy are either tools that can be manipulated to destroy the hero (as in *Coriolanus* or *Julius Caesar*) or they are the reminders of a world in which life goes on without heroes.

Some English Renaissance writers did experiment with the idea of domestic tragedy, most notably in *Arden of Faversham* (1592) and Thomas Heywood's *A Woman Killed with Kindness* (1603) (while the subjects are gentry and not commoners). Both plays are homiletic, demonstrating the consequences of adultery. The title page of *Arden of Faversham*, a story "ripped from the headlines," advertises it as "the lamentable and true tragedy of M. Arden of Faversham of Kent, wherein is shewed the great malice and dissimulation of a wicked woman, the insatiable desire of filthie lust, and the shameful end of all murderers." It thus implies this is a universal story as well as a true one. *A Woman Killed with Kindness* is more complex in its exploration of the manners of ordinary folk. In this case, Master Frankford punishes his wife for adultery by isolating her, "killing her with kindness," when she starves herself in her remorse and dies as an object of pity. Middle-class values triumph in both plays, in the victory of law and the emphasis on the values of temperance.

Playwrights of the eighteenth century also experimented with the idea of a domestic tragedy. George Lillo saw himself as breaking new ground in offering to the world a prose tragedy set in the world of London trade. In the prologue to his play, *The London Merchant* (1731), the tragic muse appears to declare her intentions to break with the past but also to ask forgiveness "if we attempt to show, / In artless strains, a tale of private woe, / A London 'prentice ruin'd is our theme." In the play, young George Barnwell is led astray by Millwood, who tempts him away from service to his good master, Thorowgood, the London merchant. To satisfy her desire she urges him first to steal from his master and then to murder his uncle. Millwood goes to her punishment unrepentant, but Barnwell is given a whole final act to express his remorse. In Germany, Gotthold Ephraim Lessing made his mark with his domestic drama *Miss Sara Sampson* (1755). This play begins with the premise of a woman as victim, Sara having being seduced by Lord Mellefont. The play unfolds the consequences of this act, as Sara seeks to make something of her life, only to be undone by the revenge of Lady Marwood, who wants Mellefont for herself. While *The London Merchant* devotes its last act to Barnwell's pious and guilt-ridden farewell to the virtuous characters of the play, *Sara Sampson* ends with Sara's agonized and drawn-out stage death by poison, meant to both horrify and thrill the audience (see Richter). Both plays were wildly successful and spawned imitators but, as Jeffrey Cox has argued, their true afterlife was in the melodrama that came to rule the European stages in the next century (411–34).

In the latter part of the nineteenth century, Émile Zola proclaimed his new doctrine of naturalism in the novel and theater. A naturalistic theater was one meant to show life exactly as it was, without apparent art, as if it were under the scientist's microscope: life as it was naturally lent itself to the tragic representation of lower-class characters, usually driven to ruin by their work and their poverty. However, in this theater, the notion of the "hero" as the exceptional individual tended to recede in the face of the grim determinism of this view of human existence. Gerhardt Hauptmann's *The Weavers* (1892) takes as its subject a Silesian weavers' revolt in 1844. It depicts in great detail the miserable lives of the workers, but it does not have a sole protagonist as the focus of the story of resistance. John M. Synge's *Riders to the Sea* (1902) evokes the tragedy endemic to a society that must live and die by the sea. If destiny in *The Weavers* is in the socioeconomic condition of the workers, here it is in the force of nature, but in both plays there is no vision of another, transcendent world.

In contrast, in the realist theater of Ibsen, the focus is more on the experience of the individual in bourgeois society. Ibsen wrote in a letter to Moritz Prozor in 1890 that in *Hedda Gabler* he wanted "to depict human beings, human emotions, and human destinies, upon a groundwork of certain of the social conditions and principles of the present day" (1908: 440). George Steiner judges that Ibsen was one of very few playwrights who could forge tragedy in the context of modernity, in a world where God has withdrawn. So, he sees, for Ibsen's heroes tragedy is engendered less in the clash between the protagonist and external forces, and more in the protagonist's "unstable soul." In Ibsen, the conflicts are internalized, or the hero's vision collides with a society that is fundamentally at odds with it. Ibsen's heroes are often driven by an idealism which is a form of blindness, an overreaching for the man caught in a commonplace world.

When Miller thus called for a refashioning of the "tragedy of the common man," a long line of playwrights stretched before him, a tradition of writers seeking to find the tragic in the everyday world. What Miller thought to be the consistent theme in the idea of tragic heroism, running from Orestes to Willy Loman, was the type of the "character who is ready to lay down his life, if need be, to secure one thing – his sense of personal dignity." It could be argued that Willy Loman, in

Death of a Salesman (1949), is the antitype of the heroic rebel and the overreacher. As Raymond Williams describes him, Loman is conformist, the type of society itself: "He brings tragedy down on himself, not by opposing the lie, but by living it" (104). When Biff, Willy's son, protests that his father has "no character," Loman's wife protests that this is not the point: "I don't say he's a great man. Willy Loman never made a lot of money. His name was never in the paper. He's not the finest character that ever lived. . . . But he's a human being, and a terrible thing is happening to him. So attention must be paid" (56). The paradigm evoked is that of a hero as Everyman from the medieval morality play, whose suffering is an emblem for all of our pain. The question remains of how to reconcile the tradition of the tragic hero as the exceptional human being who represents our aspirations in going beyond all our dreams and the idea that the everyday action of simply being human in itself holds tragic possibilities.

CHAPTER 5

Tragic History and Tragic Future

In Shakespeare's *Antony and Cleopatra*, the defeated Cleopatra imagines a future in which her story will be performed in the streets of Rome to an audience of "mechanic slaves":

> The quick comedians
> Extemporally will stage us, and present
> Our Alexandrian revels: Antony
> Shall be brought drunken forth, and I shall see
> Some squeaking Cleopatra boy my greatness
> In th'posture of a whore. (5.2.216–21)

Shakespeare's queen can see herself both living in her present grand moment in history and diminished into the subject of a future play. Ironically, that performance would happen in multiple futures: from the perspective inside the play, in an immediate future in Rome, but also in a present for Shakespeare's audience, a staging at the Globe Theatre, with the heroine played by some "squeaking Cleopatra boy." Shakespeare's history of Rome and Egypt was thus present in the world of seventeenth-century London, but for the audience in the twenty-first-century theater, where Cleopatra is played by a woman, we feel at a double distance from Cleopatra's prescient moment of impending death.

This chapter returns to where this book began, with tragedy's performance in time and its significance in history. From its beginning, tragedy was produced out of a tension between the past and present. Greek tragedy represented the figures of legend for the citizens of Athens. In the words of Vernant and Vidal-Naquet,

For the city this legendary world constitutes the past – a past sufficiently distant for the contrast between the mythical traditions that it embodies and the new forms of legal and political thought to be clearly visible; yet a past still close enough for the clash of values still to be a painful one and for this clash still to be currently taking place.

So, for example, in *Oedipus the King*, the king of ancient Thebes, who speaks in the rhythms of the language of fifth-century Athens, confronts a chorus of men singing in the old meter, who measure the king by contemporary stands and values (9–10). Comedy lives in the present because its characters so often have no history. Comic characters can thus constantly reinvent themselves. In contrast, tragic characters are bound by their own histories, but they also still live in the present of their performance, in the world the playwright has fashioned for them.

This chapter considers "tragic history" in two senses: tragedy as a representation of history and tragedy as an art form embedded in history. Tragic playwrights have always been drawn to history as the source for their stories, but when they have, how have they transformed history? In turn, how has tragedy been engaged with social and civic life? Philosophy and psychoanalysis tend to treat tragedy as representing universal human nature, yet each play was written at a particular time and place, and its meaning is deeply rooted in its language, its social milieu, and the politics of its time. The challenge is to find the link between the meaning embedded in history and the one that lives with us now. The book will end with some speculation on how tragedy will survive in this century, given its complex place in time. Can the old plays still work for us? And can a fragmented culture still produce a tragic art that draws people together?

History as Tragedy

Aristotle was the first to formulate the distinction between tragedy and history, insisting that "the poet's job is not to report what has happened but what is likely to happen: that is, what is capable of happening according to the rule of probability or necessity" (32, 1451a35). So "poetry is a more philosophical and serious business than history; for poetry speaks more of universals [*katholou*], history of particulars [*kath'hekaston*]" (33, 1451b5). Tragic poets do not need to tell things exactly as they occurred, but they are bound by a different kind of necessity, which is the likelihood of events. Aristotle's idea of probability is based on his belief in the universality of human behavior. For him, tragedy should represent not how people actually behaved in certain circumstances in the past, but how they are likely to behave, or how events are likely to transpire, if we assume that people can be counted on to behave in predictable ways (women like typical women, slaves like slaves).

Later commentators on tragedy took this idea a step further to assert tragedy's moral superiority to history. Actual events of life are not always morally edifying, but poets can fashion things as they see fit. In his *Defence of Poesy* (1959), Philip Sidney positioned the historian as inferior to the poet and philosopher, since the historian "is so tied, not to what should be but to what is, to the particular truth of things and not to the general reason of things, that his example draweth no necessary consequence" (90). Tragedy can teach virtue more effectively than history, for "if evil men come to stage, they ever go out . . . so manacled as they little animate folks to follow them. But the historian, being captived to the truth of a foolish world, is many times a terror from well-doing, and an encouragement to unbridled wickedness" (93–4). Indeed, history is full of unhappy and unedifying examples of the punishment of the virtuous and the reward of the wicked.

For the most part, Greek and Roman tragedy staged "history" from a far distant past that mixed with the world of myth. In these plays, in Argos and Thebes, gods appeared among men and women, and the characters of the heroic epics spoke and interacted with the people of the city. Rarely (except in the case of plays like Aeschylus' *Persians* or some of the Roman republican tragedies) did a play survive that staged a more recent past, a history tied more tightly to the present. When tragedy was reborn in Italy in the Renaissance (in its passage through Seneca) it seized more readily on the recent past. Mussato's *Ecerinis* played out the life of Ezzelino da Romano as a warning to the citizens of Padua. We mostly remember Ezzelino today because Dante placed him in his *Inferno* as a type of tyrant. But this play prophesied the future of tragedy, because it linked the image of the Senecan tyrant with what people would have recognized as recent history (at least that of the previous hundred years). Ezzelino is a spectacular figure, whom his mother recollects as the progeny of the devil; he professes his allegiance to the classical Furies as well as his hatred of Christ. But he was also a real man, whose presence was still felt in his city very differently from that of legendary ones.

In English Renaissance tragedy, the line between tragedy and history as a genre was easily confused. We know from Polonius in *Hamlet* that in this period differentiating genres was a messy business, since he allows not only for tragedy and comedy, but also for the "tragical historical" and the "tragical-comical-historical-pastoral." To add to the confusion, in a quarto version *Hamlet* itself is called "The Tragicall Historie of Hamlet, Prince of Denmark." In the First Quarto of *King Lear* (printed in 1608), the play was called the "True Chronicle Historie, of the life and death of King Lear and his three daughters." However, in the First Folio edition printed in 1623, it became "The Tragedie of King Lear." Even while the texts of the two plays differ, they are not so different that we can readily explain the change in title. However, the alteration does make sense when we recognize that in the First Folio the list of the "histories" includes what we think of as the first and second tetralogies, lined up in historical order (with *King John* and *Henry VIII* added). These are the plays of relatively recent British history realigned. When it was first published in a quarto edition, *Richard II* also was a "tragedy," as was *Richard III*; in the Folio they both become the "life and death" of kings, not tragedies.

It does make a difference whether you see a Shakespeare play as a tragedy or as a history. As a tragedy, a play like *Richard II* or *Richard III* is the story of one man and his rise and fall. In this context, it is his story, with a beginning, middle, and end. If you see each play as a "history" – or as a "life and death" – it becomes part of a longer story, spread out over time. In the case of Shakespeare's histories, they are part of the epic sweep from the time of the catastrophe caused by the abdication of Richard II to the victory of Henry VII over Richard III, establishing the triumphal reign of the Tudors. In this providential history, indeed, there can be no true tragedy, because all the broils, deaths, and sorrow have their end in the happy ascension of Elizabeth I to the throne of England.

Unlike the English histories, Shakespeare's Roman plays represent a distant past, and a world alien from Shakespeare's own. Tragedy was the genre marked to depict the careers of men such as Julius Caesar and Coriolanus. Their worlds hold little sense of a providential history that could transform the meaning of their own lives in the way it does for Shakespeare's kings. *Julius Caesar* stages the lives of great men who cannot see the consequences of their own momentous actions, even in an environment that drips with omens and foreboding. Only Antony knows how to manipulate events to produce the future that he desires, in his revenge for the death of Caesar and the establishment of his own power. Like Brutus (while very different in character), Coriolanus is a man out of place and time, and he becomes a casualty of a political culture that cannot tolerate him as it moves forward.

The Shakespeare play that most profoundly questions the link between history and tragedy is *Antony and Cleopatra*. The First Folio includes *Antony and Cleopatra* among the tragedies, but this play covers twelve years of Roman imperial history involving thirty-nine named characters plus hordes of soldiers and servants. The action spans vast reaches of space, across the globe from Rome to Alexandria to Tarsus in Asia Minor. The play wildly violates the unities of time, place, and action, not because Shakespeare didn't know any better (since textual evidence suggests that he knew the Countess of Pembroke's translation of Robert Garnier's *Tragedy of Antony*, as well as Samuel Daniel's closet drama of *The Tragedy of Cleopatra*, both of which observe the neoclassical rules). In this case Shakespeare seems directly defiant in pitting tragedy against history. He deletes and expands historical events to highlight his characters and themes: for example, adding Antony's campaign against the Parthians to heighten the image of his decline and inventing the character of Enobarbus as a foil to Antony.

Such changes all point to the play's breaking away from history as it explores the relationship between history and imagination, art, and theater. Antony and Cleopatra struggle to escape the trap that history has set for them. Gripped by her own vision of Antony as a man who transcends all others, a man whose "legs bestrid the ocean; his reared arms crested the world," Cleopatra dreams of a world in which they escape history. She asks Dolabella if there might ever be such a man as she has dreamt of, and when Dolabella replies "Gentle madam, no," Cleopatra protests: "Nature wants stuff / To vie strange forms with fancy; yet t'imagine / An Antony were nature's piece 'gainst fancy, / Condemning shadows quite" (5.2.97–100). If Egypt is the world of the imagination, and Rome represents the relentless march of history's reality, the two meet together in *Antony and Cleopatra* to produce tragedy, and the play dramatizes the making of that history into tragedy. In *Antony and Cleopatra* tragedy emerges from the heroes' inability to elude what really happened or what must happen.

While neoclassical tragedy tended to return to the distant past of the ancient or biblical world for its subject matter, Romantic tragedy repossessed European history, most pointedly as a reference for the present. Often writers played very loosely with the facts to convey their themes of rebellion, tyranny, love, and honor. In the late eighteenth century Friedrich Schiller composed impressive historical tragedies that explored critical political issues in his own time, including *Don Carlos* (1787), *Maria Stuart* (1800), and *Wallenstein* (1799). Schiller himself was a good enough historian to be granted a chair in history at the University of Jena, but like Shakespeare in his tragedies he manipulated history and invented events to shape his broader political themes concerned with religious conflict and the nature of authority. Schiller's heroes are above all obsessed with matters more of Schiller's time, and especially moral and political freedom. In contrast, Victor Hugo's representations of Spanish and Italian history, while they have some reference to real people, are not about the effects of history, whether of the far or recent past. As Hugo wrote in the Preface to *Cromwell*, the historian is concerned "with the exact sequence of general facts, the order of dates, the great mass movements, the battle, the conquests, the divisions of empire, the whole exterior of history"; but drama "takes the interior" (2004: 31) His plays show the characters that feel caught up in historical forces, but they are compelling in their psychological manifestations. History in these plays is more about aura than fact – an imagined other world in which heroes play out their very contemporary passions.

Tragedy in History

After the catastrophe of World War II, Bertolt Brecht issued a manifesto that called for a new theater that would match the needs of a new "scientific age" that had produced both marvels and horrors. In his "A Short Organum for the Theatre" (1948), Brecht railed against what he called the "bourgeois narcotics business," a theater where the audience submits to the action played for them as if in a trance. He was most incensed about the seductions of tragedy, the temptations of the art of a past age:

The theatre as we know it shows the structure of society (represented on the stage) as incapable of being influenced by society (in the auditorium). Oedipus, who offended against certain principles underlying the society of his time, is executed: the gods see to that; they are beyond criticism. Shakespeare's great solitary figures, bearing on their breast the star of their fate, carry through with irresistible force their futile and deadly outburst; they prepare their own downfall; life, not death, becomes obscene as they collapse; the catastrophe is beyond criticism. Human sacrifices all round! Barbaric delights! We know the barbarians have their art. Let us create another. (189)

For Brecht, tragedy was an outmoded artifact of the past that was trapped by its belief in destiny. He wanted an art for his own time that would not represent "everyman" but rather "historical man," a man represented in time who has the power to change his time rather than being bound by "historical conditions." As he pointed out, historical conditions are not "mysterious powers." Rather, "they are created and maintained by men (and will in due course be altered by them)" (190). If *Antony and Cleopatra* is a tragedy born out of the effort to escape history, for Brecht, theater should show that the forces of history can be altered by action in the present.

In *Mother Courage and Her Children* (1939), Brecht wanted to create a protagonist who could make a choice to resist but instead capitulates to suffering and refuses to change. The play follows the career of Mother Courage, a camp follower in the Thirty Years War, as she experiences the fortunes of the war and loses her three children. Brecht was particularly sensitive that he would be seen to "heroize" Mother Courage. He knew that audiences first reacted to her as a kind of universal "mother figure" and he complained of the tendency of the "bourgeois press to speak of a Niobe tragedy and of the overwhelming strength of the mother animal" (115). So he took steps to coarsen her character, suggesting that she cares more about money than about her children. No matter how hard he tried, however, Mother Courage seems to escape the contingencies in which he tried to confine her, since audiences continue to respond to her above all as the archetypal mother who suffers for her young.

The question Brecht confronted in *Mother Courage* still haunts the criticism of tragedy: what does it mean to read tragedy both with and against history? Brecht insisted that no work of art could be said to transcend the conflicts of society:

Some people may feel this to be degrading, because they rank art, once the money side has been settled, as one of the highest things; but mankind's highest decision are in fact fought out on earth, not in the heavens; in the "external world", not inside people's heads. . . . Thus for art to be "unpolitical" means only to ally itself with the "ruling" group. (196)

But Brecht's own experience with plays such as *Mother Courage* proves that tragedies will speak to us in our own moment, even though they cannot be detached from the time of their making.

It is this tension that Robert Weimann defined in an influential essay, "Past Significance and Present Meaning in Literary History," which traces the transition of historicist criticism and aesthetic theory going back to Vico, through Goethe and Schiller, Marxist and nine-teenth-century positivist criticism, to the present. Weimann argues that we do not have to choose between the values of past significance and present meaning, seeing "the past in the present but also the present in the past. Hence the 'timeless' would result through a sense of time and history" (109). Tragedy is particularly vulnerable to a contest about present vs. past meaning, insofar as tragedy has long been associated with universals of human behavior and transcendent values (Williams: 25; also Grady). Whose story *is* that of tragedy? Is it the human story, or rather, human essentials expressed from the cata-strophic confrontation with history?

Let us consider two examples of what a tragedy might look like from an "essentialist" or "universal" reading in contrast to an historical one. We can start with that play that Aristotle treated as the paradig-matic Greek tragedy: *Oedipus the King*. The first time a modern reader might know of Oedipus would not be through reading the play itself but rather through the idea of the "Oedipus complex." Apparently everyone knows that a person who has an "Oedipus complex" is in love with his mother and thus resents his father. For Freud, Sophocles' play and the legend of Oedipus corroborate the truth of the Oedipus complex, just as "the profound and universal validity of the old legends is explicable only by an equally universal validity of the above-mentioned hypothesis of infantile psychology." For Freud, the play is a tragedy of fate, which moves us inexplicably even though we may no longer believe in the power of the gods. If it does move us, it is because of this particular story:

His fate moves us only because it might have been our own, because the oracle laid upon us before our birth the very curse which rested upon him. It may be that we were all destined to direct our first sexual impulses toward our mothers, and our first impulses of hatred and violence toward our fathers; our dreams convince us that we were. King Oedipus, who slew his father Laius and wedded his mother Jocasta, is nothing more or less than a wish-fulfillment – the fulfillment of the wish of our childhood. . . . We recoil from the person for whom this primitive wish of our childhood has been fulfilled with all the force of the repression which these wishes have undergone in our minds since childhood. As the poet brings the guilt of Oedipus to light by his investigation, he forces us to become aware of our own inner selves, in which the same impulses are still extant, even though they are suppressed. . . . this admonition touches us and our own pride, we who, since the years of our childhood, have grown so wise and so powerful in our own estimation. Like Oedipus, we live in ignorance of the desires that offend morality, the desires that nature has forced upon us and after their unveiling we may well prefer to avert our gaze from the scenes of our childhood. (159–61)

In Freud's reading the Oedipus story exerts power over us, just as the oracle exercises power over Oedipus himself, because his story is our story (or rather the story of all men). All differences between the mythic places of Thebes and the terrains of our modern lives evaporate in the enactment of the tale of a man who must live to act out primal human impulses. More broadly, moving out from the story of our desires and sexual impulses, for many readers *Oedipus the King* is the story of the necessary downfall of man who tries to escape the destiny that the gods have willed for him. The message of the play is that, the more we struggle to defy those faceless demons, we must live out those stories that have been written for us, no matter how terrible they might be.

In contrast to Freud, the reading of *Oedipus the King* offered by Bernard Knox in *Oedipus at Thebes* moves us away from inner impulses to social imperatives. Knox argues against anyone's idea that this is a tragedy of fate, insisting in turn that instead "in the play which Sophocles wrote the hero's will is absolutely free and he is fully responsible for the catastrophe" (5). But Knox argues this not just to make the opposite claim for the universal nature of free will. Rather he reads the play this way because he connects it to its creation for the city of Athens. If it is a play which represents ancient Thebes, it is not really a play about the past. As Knox notes, all Greek tragedy is full of anachronisms, and *Oedipus the King* is rife with contemporary references (62). The play lived in the present of Athens as much as in the mythic world or Thebes, or, as Freud would claim, in the depths of the psyche. It was created in a specific historical moment, in a city that exercised a kind of tyrannical power over the Greek world. Oedipus was fashioned to reflect to Athens an image of itself. If it resonates with us still today, it is because of our own inheritance from Athenian culture and the way that our culture is reflected in the Athenian/Theban mirror. In the end, Knox acknowledges that "Oedipus is a paradigm of all mankind and of the city which is man's greatest creation" (195). But to say that he is an example or "para-deigma" is not to say that he is a universal figure in the way that Freud suggests. Rather, an example, or a paradigm, is a counter-image of ourselves that we also recognize as different.

Current interpretations of *Oedipus the King* and Greek tragedy call on many modes of meaning. Jean-Pierre Vernant in particular has influenced many readers of Greek tragedy in focusing on its function as a "social institution" as well as an "art form." Tragedy was more than just a mirror of that society; it was part of it, even as it called the values of that society into question (9). Some scholars have critiqued various aspects of Vernant's model (see, for example, Gould and Gold-hill in *Tragedy and the Tragic*), in particular insisting that we pay more attention to the ritual function of tragedy in Greek society. One can respond that Vernant implies that Greek tragedy embodies the tensions and conflicts inherent to the emerging polis or city state in *all* its dimensions – including the religious or ritual, filtered through the audience's and author's understanding of their place in process of change (see also Euben).

In its transmission through the centuries, tragedy became stripped of its civic roots. Many commentators have noted that Aristotle seems to have deliberately avoided linking tragedy to the city: the *Poetics* makes no mention of its role in civic life or ritual. In severing it from history, the *Poetics* made tragedy "accessible to 'everyman,' precisely because its reader is encouraged to assess tragedy in complete dissocia-tion from civic concepts" (Hall: 305). But in Western democracies, we recognize that many of our civic ideals originated in the Athenian *polis*, and its conflicts still concern us. We still struggle with the tensions between the needs and desires of the individual and the common good and the love and fear of freedom, and we too recognize the human potential for evil as well as virtue.

Like *Oedipus the King*, *Hamlet* is a play that has lent itself to constant reinterpretation. As Margreta De Grazia has written, *Hamlet* is *"timeless in value precisely because he is found timely by each successive age. He remains perennially at the vanguard of the contemporary, anticipating back in 1600 the cutting edge of the most recent now"* (355). For example, *Hamlet* has also been subjected to much psychoanalytical decoding. Freud himself suggested that

> Another of the great creations of tragic poetry, Shakespeare's *Hamlet*, has its roots in the same soil as *Oedipus Rex*. But the changed treatment of the same material reveals the whole difference in the mental life of these two widely separated epochs of civilization: the secular advance of repression in the emotional life of mankind. In Oedipus the child's wishful fantasy that underlies it is brought into the open and realized as it would be in a dream. In Hamlet it remains repressed; and – just as in the case of neurosis – we only learn of its existence from its inhibiting consequences. (298)

Curiously, Freud points to the fact of historical difference ("two widely separated epochs of civilization") in comparing Oedipus and Hamlet, even while he collapses them together as much the same character, having "roots in the same soil."

But it did not take Freud to set up Hamlet as a kind of universal type of human suffering. Samuel Taylor Coleridge observed:

> I believe the character of Hamlet may be traced to Shakespere's deep and accurate science in mental philosophy. Indeed, that this character must have some connection with the common fundamental laws of our nature may be assumed from the fact, that Hamlet has been the darling of every country in which the literature of England has been fostered. In order to understand him, it is essential that we should reflect on the constitution of our own minds. (343)

In his famous essay, "Hamlet and His Problems" (1922), T. S. Eliot noted acerbically that

> Hamlet the character has had an especial temptation for that most dangerous type of critic: the critic with a mind which is naturally of the

creative order, but which through some weakness in creative power exercises itself in criticism instead. These minds often find in Hamlet a vicarious existence for their own artistic realization. (95)

As Coleridge insisted, to find Hamlet, we should look in ourselves – even if the self you find is a literary critic.

For many critics, Hamlet is indeed the transhistorical type of intellectual, the man who thinks too much, or as the screen announces at the beginning of Laurence Olivier's film of *Hamlet*, the play is the tragedy of "a man who cannot make up his mind." A. C. Bradley marveled at the way in which "There were no old truths for Hamlet" (98). In *The Question of Hamlet*, Harry Levin saw himself in Hamlet's image. "We are Hamlet," Levin declared: "His circumstances are ours, to the extent that every man, in some measure, is born to privilege and anxiety, committed where he has never been consulted, hemmed in on all sides by an overbearing situation, and called upon to perform what must seem an ungrateful task" (43). The modern academic, beset by both "privilege and anxiety," may hardly be an "everyman," but this is one of many ways in which Hamlet's story was made modern (see Kerrigan).

But by the second half of the twentieth century, history came to *Hamlet*. In 1984 Roland Mushat Frye's *The Renaissance Hamlet* set Hamlet solidly in the world of 1600. Since then, Frye's old historicism has given way to a new historical reading of *Hamlet* as a "turn-of-the-century text" reflecting the anxieties of its age. Most recently, *Hamlet* has been seen as deeply engaged with contemporary religious controversies. Stephen Greenblatt's *Hamlet in Purgatory* uses *Hamlet* as a base to explore the notion of purgatory in Shakespeare's time. If, for Freud, the ghost is the powerful after-image of the father who is Hamlet's rival, in Greenblatt's reading the appearance of the ghost evokes the problematic status of a Catholic purgatory in Protestant England. Not only does the ghost bring with him the Senecan drive to vengeance from another time and place, but he also carries the resonance of a forbidden idea of a "communion with the dead." This Hamlet, burdened with the pressure of contesting religious ideologies, is simply not the same man who thinks too much.

Yet, just as the Oedipus who is the image of Athens is also an Oedipus that we recognize because of our complex cultural and political inheritance from that world, the Renaissance Hamlet, produced by a society still divided by religious strife and doubt, is a character both alien and knowable. And even while we may not respond to the particular qualities of Hamlet's religious doubt, we can understand his tremendous fear of all that is unknown. We also still feel deeply the great sense of waste, for all the souls lost at the play's end, but most of all for Hamlet, who has carried us with him in his desperate effort to know how to do what is right. Tragedy indeed does not make us choose between an emotional and visceral response and an awareness of difference. Instead, it deepens our understanding of the past and of our own lives.

Tragic Future

In 1961, in the aftermath of World War II and in the midst of the Cold War, George Steiner announced the death of tragedy. Tragedy has become impossible in our time, he argued, for two fundamental reasons. First, there has been a coarsening or what he calls a "stiffening of the bone" in our imaginations and our very language, emptied out by a century of atrocities:

> Each day we sup our fill of horrors – in the newspaper, on the television screen, or the radio – and thus we grow insensible to fresh outrage. This numbness has a crucial bearing on the possibility of tragic style. . . . Compared with the realities of war and oppression that surround us, the gravest imaginings of the poets are diminished to a scale of private or artificial terror. (315)

Certainly, other centuries could match the twentieth in its terrors. However, that century differed from earlier ones in the ways we came to know that horror. Before film, television, and the internet, newspapers and broadsides reported the sufferings of others, but that news was relayed mostly as text. Now, through the media, not only are we exposed to a scale of global suffering unimaginable before television and the internet, but we also see it represented before us in images that mime the effects of the theater. People in the developed world may be protected from the real experience of death in their own communities or lives, when death takes place behind closed doors, but we see murder and mayhem, real or imagined, on our screens on a daily basis. How can we not be numb to them?

Further, Steiner argues, tragedy is impossible in our time because we lack the kind of shared culture, mythology, and theology that sustained the Greek and Elizabethan theater. The Greek and Elizabethan tragic theaters were public in the best sense, a "popular culture" (though they do not look anything to us like what we recognize as popular culture in our own time). Greek tragedy was perhaps the most radical version of popular culture, in that the annual performances at the Theatre of Dionysus would be attended by so many citizens. While Elizabethan theater was less inclusive, for the citizens of London it was still fundamentally an open theater – if you had a penny to spend. According to Steiner, the audience that would attend that theater shared roughly the same beliefs. The Greeks had their magical gods and their sense of destiny, and the Elizabethans a Christian world that was equally terrifying and mysterious. But that world gave way to one of reason, and, writes Steiner, "the myths which have prevailed since Descartes and Newton are myths of reason, no truer perhaps than those which preceded them, but less responsive to the claims of art. Yet when it is torn loose from the mooring of myth, art tends toward anarchy" (321).

In response, Raymond Williams adamantly opposes the assumption that there can be no such thing as "modern tragedy" because "our philosophical assumptions are non-tragic." Instead, he argues, the forms of thinking that dominated the twentieth century – Marxism, Freudianism, Existentialism – are inherently tragic in form:

> Man can achieve his full life only after violent conflict; man is essentially frustrated and divided against himself. While he lives in society; man is torn by intolerable contradictions, in a condition of essential absurdity. From these ordinary propositions, and from their combination in so many minds, it is not surprising that so much tragedy has in fact emerged. (189)

Indeed, one can see that these ideas shaped much of the tragic drama of the twentieth century in the West, especially when playwrights turned to the old stories. In particular, psychoanalysis underwrote the tragedies of Eugene O'Neill: his *Mourning Becomes Electra* (1931) set the essential plot and themes of the *Oresteia* as a tangled web of sexual betrayal, incest, and repression in nineteenth-century America. And in turn, Existentialism informed Jean-Paul Sartre's transformations of the *Oresteia*, in *The Flies* (1943).

In the twentieth century, playwrights clearly believed they could make the old plays live again in the context of new myths. Besides Sartre, other French playwrights had turned to the classics to stage modern tragedy: Cocteau in his *Antigone* (1922) and *La Machine infernale* (1934) (based on the Oedipus story), and Giraudoux in his *Amphitryon 38* (1929), *The Trojan War Will Not Take Place* (1935), and *Électra* (1937). During World War II, the emulation of Greek tragedy provided both the thematic material and a screen for playwrights handling political material. If O'Neill's version of the *Oresteia* extracted family angst from the story, Sartre's *The Flies* used the story to grapple with the power of blood guilt and cowardice during the French occupation. Jean Anouilh's version of *Antigone* (1944), produced during the occupation, is a profoundly ambivalent study of political defiance and capitulation.

This recourse to the classics may have run its course. As Camus said, the public can become "tired of the Atridae, of adaptations from antiquity, of that modern tragic sense which, alas, is all too rarely present in ancient myths however generously they may be stuffed with anachronisms" (cited in Williams: 209). It was not only the modern European West that turned to the old plays. They have reappeared in the culture of Africa and the Caribbean, if never without a sense of irony and difference. Wole Soyinka's *Bacchae* (1973) is the play that most explicitly evokes Greek tragedy, transfiguring Euripides' play in the political context of both the post-colonial moment and Yoruba myth. Other African playwrights like Ola Rotimi, in his *The Gods Are Not to Blame* (1968), a reworking of *Oedipus the King*, also use the old plays to consciously criticize the ground of Western tragedy as they re-create it (see Reiss, in *Companion to Tragedy*).

Steiner's judgment of the failure of contemporary life, and thus of contemporary tragedy, is of course profoundly conservative. It is driven by the sense of the poverty, rather than the possibilities, of our lives and our world, which are fragmented, diverse, and contingent. But Williams's counter-argument for the vitality of the new myths of the twentieth century – Marxism, Freudian thought, and Existentialism – may no longer hold true either. Freudian ideas may still have a hold on the popular idea of what drives our behavior, but in psychology those ideas have largely given way to a new debate over the balance between the genetic and environmental factors that govern what we do. Marxism has lost much of its political currency in the face of an evolving global economy. Now, more than ever, instead we struggle to find our way over a shifting ground of belief, with extremes of fundamentalism on the one side and skepticism on the other.

But it is important to remember that in fact neither fifth-century Athens nor early modern London were the kind of unified society, with a shared system of belief that Steiner would have us think. Certainly, both cities that produced the greatest tragic theater were themselves in the midst of radical change. Tragedy could never emerge in the context of stasis or self-satisfaction, because it is a genre that rises out of the fissures of belief, authority, law, and social convention. In both societies, Greek and Elizabethan, the state wanted to promulgate religious and social orthodoxy, but anytime this happens you can be sure that the state has something to prove, and a situation that it feels it needs to control. The fifth-century Athenian city-state felt threatened from both inside and outside: from inside, by those not granted the identity of citizens – women, slaves, metics (or resident aliens), and from outside, from threats from the East and from its rival cities in the Mediterranean. In early modern London, religious division was still rife, and the government feared treason from within and invasion from without, instigated by European Catholic powers. There was also a pervasive sense of economic instability stimulated by new capitalistic practices and the discoveries in the New World. Given this picture of the past, it could be argued that there is no better time than now for the production of tragedy, in a world that feels the ground shifting under it so profoundly, and where what one believes once again matters so much and so few can agree about their beliefs.

Perhaps, as Steiner has argued, our world is too fragmented now to sustain a tragic theater, because live theater is no longer the lifeblood of our civic culture. It has given way to the multiplicity of "screen" forms of represented reality that used to be the province of the theater alone (as opposed to the novel). Many cultural observers have argued that film has taken over the role that theater used to play as a popular art (and of course that film has pulled away the audience from theater). In turn, cinema is now seen to be threatened, first by television and then by all the forms of screen pleasures that are available on your computer monitor. The screen experience is increasingly a solitary one. In the tragic theater we are rarely allowed to encounter the actor alone, not in relationship to others, whereas in film, discontinuity, and thus isolation is possible. Tragic theater is thus inherently communal and social in a way that is not necessarily true for film. The implication is that, except for a small fraction of people, we will lose the communal experience that tragedy enacted live.

But the global market in film and image and the internet do enable a new cultural communality. Paradoxically, the same technologies that have increased cultural fragmentation through the proliferation of unimaginably diverse kinds of music, art, and film have also produced new ways of sharing art: an image or text can be instantly downloaded by people around the world. The power of this technology has mostly lent itself to the circulation of the cheap fragment of horror, comedy, or scandal, but it does hold great potential for the future of a new democratic art and thus the art of tragedy. In the developed world, it may appear that a large percentage of the population is locked away into the private world channeled through their headphones, cell phones, or ipods. But at the same time, artists and writers are producing new forms of narrative and screen art, for a global audience. Who can say what sort of tragic art will emerge?

Plays Cited

The following is a list of editions of all plays discussed from which citations are made. All Shakespeare plays are from the Riverside edition unless noted otherwise.

Aeschylus (1985). *The Oresteia*, trans. Robert Fagles. New York: Penguin.

Aeschylus (1942). *Prometheus Bound*, trans. David Grene. In *Aeschylus* Vol. 2. Chicago: University of Chicago Press.

Anouilh, Jean (1958). *Antigone*, trans. Lewis Galantière. In *Jean Anouilh: Five Plays*, Vol. 1. New York: Hill & Wang.

Arden of Faversham (1973). Ed. M. L. Wine. London: Methuen.

Aristophanes (1969). *The Frogs*, trans. Richmond Lattimore. In *Four Comedies*, ed. William Arrowsmith. Ann Arbor: University of Michigan Press.

Beckett, Samuel (1982). *Waiting for Godot*. New York: Grove Press.

Corneille, Pierre (1976). *The Cid, Cinna, The Theatrical Illusion*, ed. John Cairncross. New York: Penguin.

Eliot, T. S. (1935). *Murder in the Cathedral*. New York: Harcourt, Brace.

Euripides (1955). *The Medea*. In *Euripides*, Vol. 1, ed. David Grene and trans. Richmond Lattimore. Chicago: University of Chicago Press.

Euripides (1956). *Heracles*. In *Euripides*, Vol. 2, ed. David Grene and trans. Richmond Lattimore. Chicago: University of Chicago Press.

Euripides (1978). *The Bakkhai*, trans. Robert Bagg. Amherst: University of Massachusetts Press.

Heywood, Thomas (1971). *A Woman Killed with Kindness*. Menston: Scolar Press.

Hugo, Victor (2004). *Four Plays*, ed. Claude Schumacher. London: Methuen.

Ibsen, Henrik (1992). *Four Major Plays*, Vol. 1, trans. Rolf Fjelde. New York: New American Library.

Jonson, Ben (1999). *Sejanus*. In *Five Plays*, ed. G. A. Wilkes. New York: Oxford University Press.

Kyd, Thomas (1989). *The Spanish Tragedy*, ed. J. R. Mulryne. New York: W. W. Norton.

Lillo, George (1965). *The London Merchant*, ed. William H. McBurney. London: Edward Arnold.

Marlowe, Christopher (1969). *The Complete Plays*, ed. J. B. Steane. New York: Penguin.

Marlowe, Christopher (2005). *Doctor Faustus: A Two-Text Edition (A-Text, 1604; B-Text, 1616); Contexts and Sources; Criticism*, ed. David Scott Kastan. New York: W. W. Norton.

Miller, Arthur (1949). *Death of a Salesman*. New York: Viking Press.

Mussato, Albertino (1975). *Ecerinis*, ed. L. Padrin. Munich: W. Fink.

Preston, Thomas (1976). *Cambyses*, in *Drama of the English Renaissance*, Vol. 1, *The Tudor Period*, ed. Russell Fraser and Norman Rabkin. New York: Prentice Hall.

Racine, Jean (1960). *Britannicus*. In *Five Plays*, trans. Kenneth Muir. New York: Hill & Wang.

Racine, Jean (1963). *Iphigenia, Phaedra, Athaliah*, trans. John Cairncross. New York: Penguin.

Racine, Jean (1996). *Phèdre*, ed. R. Parish. London: Duckworth.

Schiller, Friedrich (1980). *The Robbers and Wallenstein*, trans. F. J. Lamport. New York: Penguin.

Shakespeare, William (1997). *The Riverside Shakespeare*, 2nd edn, ed. G. Blakemore Evans. New York: Houghton Mifflin.

Shakespeare, William (2003). *The Three-Text Hamlet: Parallel Texts of the First and Second Quartos and First Folio*, 2nd edn, ed. Bernice W. Kliman and Paul Bertram. New York: AMS Press.

Sophocles (1982). *The Three Theban Plays: Antigone; Oedipus the King; Oedipus at Colonus*, intro. Bernard Knox and trans. Robert Fagles. New York: The Viking Press.

Webster, John (1983). *The White Devil*. In *The Selected Plays of John Webster*, ed. Jonathan Dollimore. New York: Cambridge University Press.

Bibliography

Aristotle (1970). *Poetics*, trans. Gerald F. Else. Ann Arbor: University of Michigan Press.

Auden, W. H. (1945). "The Christian Tragic Hero." *The New York Times Book Review*, December: BR1.

Bacon, Francis (2002). "Of Revenge." In *The Major Works*, ed. Brian Vickers. New York: Oxford University Press, 347–8.

Bacon, Helen H. (1994/5). "The Chorus in Greek Life and Drama." *Arion: A Journal of Humanities and the Classics*, 3.1, 6–24.

Barthes, Roland (1964). *On Racine*, trans. Richard Howard (translation of *Sur Racine*, originally published 1960). New York: Hill & Wang.

Bazin, André (2005). "Theater and Cinema." In *Theater and Film: A Comparative Anthology*, ed. Robert Knopf. New Haven, CT: Yale University Press, 110–33.

Belsey, Catherine (1985). *The Subject of Tragedy: Identity and Difference in Renaissance Drama*. London: Methuen.

Bentley, Eric (2005). "Realism and the Cinema." In *Theater and Film: A Comparative Anthology*, ed. Robert Knopf. New Haven, CT: Yale University Press, 103–9.

Bergman, Ingmar (2005). "The Screenwriter as Auteur." In *Theater and Film: A Comparative Anthology*, ed. Robert Knopf. New Haven, CT: Yale University Press, 227–38.

Boedeker, Deborah and Kurt Raaflaub (2005). "Tragedy and City." In *A Companion to Tragedy*, ed. Rebecca Bushnell. Oxford: Blackwell, 109–27.

Booth, W. C. (1974). *A Rhetoric of Irony*. Chicago: University of Chicago Press.

Braden, Gordon (1985). *Renaissance Tragedy and the Senecan Tradition: Anger's Privilege*. New Haven, CT: Yale University Press.

Bradley, A. C. (1955). *Shakespearean Tragedy*. New York: Meridian Books.

Brecht, Bertolt (1964). *Brecht on Theatre*, ed. and trans. John Willett. New York: Hill & Wang.

Brown, John Russell (1995). *The Oxford Illustrated History of the Theatre*. New York: Oxford University Press.

Bushnell, Rebecca W. (1990). *Tragedies of Tyrants: Political Thought and Theater in the English Renaissance*. Ithaca, NY: Cornell University Press.

Bushnell, Rebecca (2005). "The Fall of Princes: The Classical and Medieval Roots of English Renaissance Tragedy." In *A Companion to Tragedy*, ed. Rebecca Bushnell. Oxford: Blackwell, 289–306.

Calame, Claude (2005). "The Tragic Choral Group: Dramatic Roles and Social Functions," trans. Dan Edelstein. In *A Companion to Tragedy*, ed. Rebecca Bushnell. Oxford: Blackwell, 215–33.

Cave, Terence (1988). *Recognitions: A Study in Poetics*. New York: Oxford University Press.

Chandler, Raymond (1955). "The Simple Art of Murder." In *Later Novels and Other Writings*. New York: Library of America, 977–92.

Chaucer, Geoffrey (1987). *The Riverside Chaucer*, 3rd edn, ed. Larry D. Benson. Boston: Houghton Mifflin. [Based on *The Works of Geoffrey Chaucer*, ed. F. N. Robinson.]

Clopper, Lawrence W. (2002). "English Drama: From Ungodly *Ludi* to Sacred Play." In *The Cambridge History of Medieval English Literature*, ed. David Wallace. Cambridge: Cambridge University Press, 739–66.

Cohen, Walter (1997). "[Introduction to Antony and Cleopatra]." In *The Norton Shakespeare*, ed. Stephen Greenblatt. New York: W. W. Norton, 2619–27.

Coleridge, Samuel Taylor (1904). "Lecture on Hamlet." In *Lectures and Notes on Shakspere and Other English Poets*. London: George Bell & Sons, 342–68.

Coleridge, Samuel Taylor (1989). "[Commentary on *Othello*]." In *Coleridge's Criticism of Shakespeare*, ed. R. A. Foakes. Detroit, MI: Wayne State University Press, 110–16.

Cox, Jeffrey (2005). "Romantic Tragic Drama and its Eighteenth-Century Precursors: Remaking British Tragedy." In *A Companion to Tragedy*, ed. Rebecca Bushnell. Oxford: Blackwell, 411–34.

d'Aubignac, François Hédelin (2001). *La pratique du théâtre*, ed. Hélène Baby. Paris: H. Champion.

De Grazia, Margreta (1997). "World Pictures, Modern Periods, and the Early Stage." In *A New History of Early English Drama*, ed. John D. Cox and David Scott Kastan. New York: Columbia University Press, 7–21.

De Grazia, Margreta (2001). "Hamlet before Its Time." *Modern Language Quarterly*, 62, 355–76.

Dollimore, Jonathan (2004). *Radical Tragedy: Religion, Ideology and Power in the Drama of Shakespeare and his Contemporaries*. Chapel Hill, NC: Duke University Press.

Eagleton, Terry (2003). *Sweet Violence: The Idea of the Tragic*. Malden, MA: Blackwell.

Eliot, T. S. (1920). "Hamlet and His Problems." In *The Sacred Wood: Essays on Poetry and Criticism*. London: Methuen, 95–103.

Euben, Peter, ed. (1986). *Greek Tragedy and Political Theory*. Berkeley: University of California Press.

Fjelde, Rolf (1992). Foreword to *Ibsen: Four Major Plays*: Vol. 1. New York: Signet.

Freud, Sigmund (1944). *The Interpretation of Dreams*, trans. A. A. Brill. New York: The Modern Library.

Frye, Northrop (1957). "Archetypal Criticism: Theory of Myths." In *Anatomy of Criticism; Four Essays*. Princeton, NJ: Princeton University Press, 131–239.

Frye, Roland (1984). *The Renaissance Hamlet: Issues and Responses in 1600*. Princeton, NJ: Princeton University Press.

Girard, René (1977). *Violence and the Sacred*. Baltimore, MD: Johns Hopkins University Press.

Goldhill, Simon (1996). "Collectivity and Otherness – The Authority of the Tragic Chorus: Response to Gould." In *Tragedy and the Tragic*, ed. M. S. Silk. Oxford: Clarendon Press, 244–56.

Goodkin, Richard (2005). "Neoclassical Dramatic Theory in Seventeenth-Century France." In *A Companion to Tragedy*, ed. Rebecca Bushnell. Oxford: Blackwell, 373–92.

Gould, John (1996). "Tragedy and Collective Experience." In *Tragedy and the Tragic*, ed. M. S. Silk. Oxford: Clarendon Press, 217–43.

Grady, Hugh (2005). "Tragedy and Materialist Thought." In *A Companion to Tragedy*, ed. Rebecca Bushnell. Oxford: Blackwell, 125–44.

Greenblatt, Stephen (2001). *Hamlet in Purgatory*. Princeton, NJ: Princeton University Press.

Greene, Robert and Henry Chettle (1994). *Greene's Groatsworth of Wit: Bought with a Million of Repentance*, ed. D. Allen Carroll. Binghamton, NY: Medieval and Renaissance Texts & Studies.

Gurr, Andrew (1996). *Playgoing in Shakespeare's London*. Cambridge: Cambridge University Press.

Hall, Edith (1996). "Is there a *Polis* in Aristotle's *Poetics?*" In *Tragedy and the Tragic: Greek Theatre and Beyond*, ed. M. S. Silk. New York: Oxford University Press, 295–309.

Halleran, Michael (2005). "Greek Tragedy in Performance." In *A Companion to Tragedy*, ed. Rebecca Bushnell. Oxford: Blackwell, 198–214.

Hegel, G. W. F. (1975). *Aesthetics: Lectures on Fine Art*, Vol. 2, trans. T. M. Knox. Oxford: Clarendon Press.

Herington, John (1985). *Poetry into Drama: Early Tragedy and the Greek Poetic Tradition*. Berkeley: University of California Press.

Howarth, William (1976). *Sublime and Grotesque: A Study of French Romantic Drama*. New York: Harrap.

Hugo, Victor (2004). *The Essential Victor Hugo*, ed. E. H. Blackmore and A. M. Blackmore. London: Oxford University Press.

Ibsen, Henrik (1908). *Letters*, trans. John Nilsen Laurvik and Mary Morison. New York: Duffield.

Ibsen, Henrik (1964). "To Edmund Gosse; Dresden, January 15, 1874." In *Letters and Speeches*. New York: Hill & Wang.

Jackson, Russell (2004). "Victorian and Edwardian Stagecraft: Techniques and Issues." In *A Cambridge Companion to Victorian and Edwardian Theatre*, ed. Kerry Powell. Cambridge: Cambridge University Press.

Johnson, Samuel (1986). "King Lear." In *Selections from Johnson on Shakespeare*, ed. Bertrand H. Bronson. New Haven, CT: Yale University Press.

Jones, John (1962). *On Aristotle and Greek Tragedy*. New York: Oxford University Press.

Kerrigan, William (1996). *Hamlet's Perfection*. Baltimore: Johns Hopkins University Press.

Knox, Bernard (1964). *The Heroic Temper*. Berkeley: University of California Press.

Knox, Bernard M. W. (1957). *Oedipus at Thebes*. New Haven, CT: Yale University Press.

Lawrenson, Thomas E. (1986). *The French Stage and Playhouse in the XVIIth Century: A Study in the Advent of the Italian Order*, 2nd edn. New York: AMS Press.

Leacroft, Richard and Helen Leacroft (1984). *Theatre and Playhouse: An Illustrated Survey of Theatre Buildings from Ancient Greece to the Present Day*. London: Methuen.

Levin, Harry (1952). *The Overreacher: A Study of Christopher Marlowe*. Boston: Beacon Press.

Levin, Harry (1959). *The Question of Hamlet*. Oxford: Oxford University Press.

Lloyd, Michael (1992). *The Agon in Euripides*. New York: Oxford University Press.

Loraux, Nicole (1987). *Tragic Ways of Killing a Woman*, trans. Anthony Forster. Cambridge, MA: Harvard University Press.

Mahelot, Laurent (1930). *Le Mémoire de Mahelot*. Paris: Champion.

Man, Glenn (2000). "Ideology and Genre in the *Godfather* Films." In *Francis Ford Coppola's The Godfather Trilogy*, ed. Nick Browne. Cambridge: Cambridge University Press.

Maskall, David (1991). *Racine: A Theatrical Reading*. Oxford: Clarendon.

Maus, Katharine Eisaman (1995). *Inwardness and Theater in the English Renaissance*. Chicago: University of Chicago Press.

McDonald, Russ (2001). *Shakespeare and the Arts of Language*. New York: Oxford University Press.

McGowan, Margaret (1982). "Racine's 'Lieu Théâtral.'" In *Form and Meaning: Aesthetic Coherence in Seventeenth-Century French Drama*, ed. William D. Howarth, Ian McFarlane, and Margaret McGowan. Aldershot: Avebury.

Miller, Arthur (1949). "Tragedy and the Common Man." *The New York Times*, February, X1-3.

Milton, John (1968). *Paradise Lost*, ed. Christopher Ricks. New York: Signet.

Mullin, Donald C. (1970). *The Development of the Playhouse: A Survey of Theatre Architecture from the Renaissance to the Present*. Berkeley and Los Angeles: University of California Press.

Murnaghan, Sheila (2005). "Women in Greek Tragedy." In *A Companion to Tragedy*, ed. Rebecca Bushnell. Oxford: Blackwell, 234–50.

Naremore, James (1998). *More Than Night: Film Noir in its Contexts*. Berkeley: University of California Press.

Neill, Michael (2005). "English Revenge Tragedy." In *A Companion to Tragedy*, ed. Rebecca Bushnell. Oxford: Blackwell, 328–50.

Nietzsche, Friedrich (1999). *The Birth of Tragedy and Other Writings*, ed. Raymond Geuss and trans. Ronald Speirs. New York: Cambridge University Press.

Peradotto, John J. (1969). "Cledonomancy in the Oresteia." *American Journal of Philology*, January, 90.1, 1–21.

Poole, Adrian (2005). *Tragedy: A Very Short Introduction*. New York: Oxford University Press.

Rackin, Phyllis (2005). *Shakespeare and Women*. Oxford: Oxford University Press.

Reiss, Timothy J. (1980). *Tragedy and Truth: Studies in the Development of a Renaissance and Neoclassical Discourse*. New Haven, CT: Yale University Press.

Reiss, Timothy J. (2005). "Using Tragedy against its Makers: Some African and Caribbean Instances." In *A Companion to Tragedy*, ed. Rebecca Bushnell. Oxford: Blackwell, 505–26.

Richter, Simon (2005). "German Classical Tragedy: Lessing, Goethe, Schiller, Kleist, and Büchner." In *A Companion to Tragedy*, ed. Rebecca Bushnell. Oxford: Blackwell, 435–51.

Rymer, Thomas (1956). "The Tragedies of the Last Age Consider'd." In *The Critical Works of Thomas Rymer*, ed. Curt A. Zimansky. New Haven, CT: Yale University Press, 17–76.

Schlegel, A. W. (1846). *Sämliche Werke V. Vorlesungen über dramatische Kunst and Literatur* [Complete Works C. Lectures on dramatic art and literature], ed. E. Böcking. Leipzig: Weidmann.

Segal, Charles (1982). *Dionysiac Poetics and Euripides' Bacchae*. Princeton, NJ: Princeton University Press.

Shaw, George Bernard (1948). "A Doll's House." In *Our Theatres in the Nineties*. London: Constable, 129–34.

Sidney, Philip (2002). *An Apology for Poetry; or, The Defence of Poesy*, 3rd edn, ed. Geoffrey Shepherd and rev. R. W. Maslen (first published 1965). New York: Manchester University Press.

Silk, M. S. (1996). "Tragic Language: The Greek Tragedians and Shakespeare." In *Tragedy and the Tragic: Greek Theatre and Beyond*, ed. M. S. Silk. New York: Oxford University Press.

Silk, M. S. and J. P. Stern (1981). *Nietzsche on Tragedy*. New York: Cambridge University Press.

Sontag, Susan (2005). "Film and Theatre." In *Theater and Film: A Comparative Anthology*, ed. Robert Knopf. New Haven, CT: Yale University Press, 134–51.

States, Bert O. (1985). *Great Reckonings in Little Rooms: On the Phenomenology of the Theater*. Berkeley and Los Angeles: University of California Press.

Steiner, George (1961). *The Death of Tragedy*. London: Faber & Faber.

Taplin, Oliver (1978). *Greek Tragedy in Action*. London: Methuen.

Vernant, Jean-Pierre and Pierre Vidal-Naquet (1988). *Myth and Tragedy in Ancient Greece*, trans. Janet Lloyd. New York: Zone Books.

Waith, Eugene M. (1962). *The Herculean Hero in Marlowe, Chapman, Shakespeare and Dryden*. New York: Columbia University Press.

Warshow, Robert (1962). *The Immediate Experience: Movies, Comics, Theatre & Aspects of Popular Culture*, intro. Lionel Trilling. New York: Atheneum.

Weimann, Robert (1969). "Past Significance and Present Meaning in Literary History." *New Literary History*, 1.1, 91–109.

Wickham, Glynne (1959). *Early English Stages[,] 1300 to 1660*. London: Routledge & Kegan Paul.

Williams, Raymond (1966). *Modern Tragedy*. Stanford, CA: Stanford University Press.

Zeitlin, Froma (1996). *Playing the Other: Gender and Society in Classical Greek Literature*. Chicago: University of Chicago Press.

Zola, Émile (1964). "Naturalism on the Stage." In *The Experimental Novel and Other Essays*, trans. Belle M. Sherman. New York: Haskell.

Index